The Learner-Centred Curriculum

THE CAMBRIDGE APPLIED LINGUISTICS SERIES

Series editors: Michael H. Long and Jack C. Richards

This series presents the findings of recent work in applied linguistics which are of direct relevance to language teaching and learning and of particular interest to applied linguists, researchers, language teachers, and teacher trainers.

In this series:

The Learner-Centred Curriculum

A study in second language teaching

David Nunan

CAMBRIDGE
UNIVERSITY PRESS

PUBLISHED BY THE PRESS SYNDICATE OF THE UNIVERSITY OF CAMBRIDGE
The Pitt Building, Trumpington Street, Cambridge, United Kingdom

CAMBRIDGE UNIVERSITY PRESS
The Edinburgh Building, Cambridge CB2 2RU, UK
40 West 20th Street, New York, NY 10011–4211, USA
10 Stamford Road, Oakleigh, VIC 3166, Australia
Ruiz de Alarcón 13, 28014 Madrid, Spain
Dock House, The Waterfront, Cape Town 8001, South Africa

http://www.cambridge.org

First published 1988
Twelfth printing 2001

Printed in the United Kingdom at the University Press, Cambridge

British Library Cataloguing in Publication data
Nunan, David
The learner-centred curriculum
1. English language – Study and teaching – Foreign
speakers   2. Curriculum planning
1. Title
428.2′4′07   PE1128.A2

Library of Congress Cataloguing in Publication data
Nunan, David
The learner-centred curriculum.
Bibliography
Includes index.
1. English language – Study and teaching – Foreign
speakers   I. Title   II. Title: Learner-centred
curriculum.
PE1128.A2N86   1988   428′.007   87–26802

ISBN 0 521 35309 2 hardback
ISBN 0 521 35843 4 paperback

To Cath
for her time, patience and support.

Contents

Series Editors' Preface

Australia has one of the largest and most dynamic migrant education language programmes in the world. What makes the Australian Adult Migrant Education Program (AMEP) unique is that although the program is co-ordinated at the national level, the process of curriculum development it embodies is bottom up rather than top down. At each institution where migrant language programs are offered, learners are actively involved in setting their own goals and determining what and how they will learn. It is this experience which Dr David Nunan, director of the National Curriculum Resource Centre, Adelaide, presents in this important book.

This is more than just an account of the AMEP however. This book offers a model of what curriculum development is. David Nunan shows that curriculum development involves the interaction of needs analysis, goal setting, grading and sequencing of content, materials development, implementation and evaluation, and shows how these processes interact within a learner-centered approach to curriculum. Throughout, the discussion is illustrated with numerous examples from the AMEP experience. At the same time, Nunan demonstrates that curriculum work must move beyond speculation and have a solid empirical basis if it is to have any substance, and illustrates the use of questionnaire, interview and case study data in curriculum planning. In addition, Nunan demonstrates that language curriculum practitioners have much to learn from mainstream educational research and practice.

The AMEP is a unique example of a national curriculum project which attributes a central role to both teachers and learners at every phase of the curriculum process. As such, it should be examined carefully by all those involved in language curriculum work. We are happy to have the opportunity to bring this important work to the attention of a wider audience through its publication in the Cambridge Applied Linguistics Series.

Michael H. Long
Jack C. Richards

Preface

This book presents curriculum theory and practice as these are applied to English language teaching. The concept of 'learner-centredness' provides a unifying theme for the work as a whole, and, while the focus of the study is adult ESL, it is hoped that the book has something to say to those working in EFL and also to those working with children.

The book takes a 'bottom-up' view of curriculum development. In other words, it is grounded in studies of what language teachers actually do and think as they plan, implement and evaluate their language programmes, rather than on what curriculum specialists say they ought to do. A series of exemplary case studies of teachers at work illustrates and reinforces the theoretical perspectives presented in the body of the book.

The book attempts to marry theoretical perspectives and empirical insights from applied linguistics with those from curriculum research and development. It is hoped that the marriage is a happy one, and that the strengths rather than the weaknesses of both disciplines are apparent in the work. It is also hoped that teachers, researchers and academics working within a linguistic paradigm might come to see the benefits to be derived from applying general educational theory and research to language teaching.

This book owes a great deal to the Australian Adult Migrant Education Program (AMEP) which is charged with the task of providing English language learning opportunities to non-English speaking immigrants to Australia. The studies in the book were only made possible by the collaboration, assistance and involvement of many of the fifteen hundred teachers employed by the AMEP. These teachers gave generously of their time and professional expertise, and the ideas and insights presented here belong to them.

While is is not possible to name all those who helped make this study possible, it would be remiss of me not to acknowledge the support and assistance of several special individuals. Foremost is Geoff Brindley who was a joint partner in the development of many of the ideas presented here. I owe a great deal to the editors of this series, Jack Richards and Mike Long, both of whom have been extremely supportive. I should also like to thank the following individuals for their encouragement, assistance and advice: Chris Candlin, Carole Urzua, Pat Rigg, Alan Beretta and Leo van Lier. Thanks are also due to my colleagues at the

National Curriculum Resource Centre, in particular to Jill Burton and Mary Szabo. Finally, I should like to thank Peter Donovan, Adrian du Plessis and Ellen Shaw from Cambridge University Press for their advice and support.

Adelaide, April 1987.

1 *Introduction*

1.1 Preamble

Traditionally 'curriculum' is taken to refer to a statement or statements of intent – the 'what should be' of a course of study. In this work a rather different perspective is taken. The curriculum is seen in terms of what teachers actually do; that is, in terms of 'what is', rather than 'what should be'. The work is thus based on what many language teachers have found both desirable and possible.

The curriculum is seen from the perspective of the teacher for two reasons. In the first place, in the sort of learner centred system towards which many language teaching organisations are moving, the teacher is the prime agent of curriculum development. Second, educational reality is not what educational planners say ought to happen, but what teachers and learners actually do. The notion that planning equals teaching and that teaching equals learning is naive. Research suggests that the equation is much more complex than this, that teachers do not slavishly follow a pre-specified plan, and that learners do not necessarily always learn what teachers teach (Allwright 1986; Burton and Nunan 1986). It is this insight which has prompted within these pages a rather different view of language curricula.

1.2 Linguistics and Language Teaching

Due to a series of events which are partly circumstantial and partly historical, much of the development in language teaching has occurred outside the educational mainstream. The assumption seems to have been that educational theory and research has very little to contribute to the field of language teaching.

The implicit message, that learning a language is so different from learning anything else that there is little point in developing links with the educational mainstream, has been partly due to the disproportionate influence exercised over the field by theoretical linguists. The belief that language pedagogy is basically a linguistic rather than an educational matter has led to research which is couched within a linguistic rather than an educational paradigm. This, in turn, has created a fragmentation

1

within the field, with different interest groups being concerned with particular aspects of the teaching–learning process to the exclusion of other aspects. Thus, in Europe, in the 1970s, the focus was on the specification of content through the development of syllabuses which had a linguistic focus. While the development of functional–notional syllabuses represented a broadened focus, the focus itself was still basically linguistic, and there was a comparative neglect of methodology. Other practitioners focused on methodology to the exclusion of other elements in the curriculum, such as content specification and evaluation.

This state of affairs is beginning to be redressed. In the last two or three years a number of publications have appeared urging the development of integrated approaches to language curriculum development. (See for example Stern 1983; Yalden 1983; Richards 1984; Nunan 1985a; Dubin and Olshtain 1986.) These publications urge the development of procedures which are systematic and comprehensive, containing similar components to those contained in traditional curriculum development.

1.3   Learner-Centred Curriculum Development

This work differs from other publications in that it provides a theoretical and empirical rationale for learner-centred curriculum development within an adult ESL context. Such a curriculum will contain similar elements to those contained in traditional curriculum development, that is, planning (including needs analysis, goal and objective setting), implementation (including methodology and materials development) and evaluation (see for example Hunkins 1980).

However, the key difference between learner-centred and traditional curriculum development is that, in the former, the curriculum is a collaborative effort between teachers and learners, since learners are closely involved in the decision-making process regarding the content of the curriculum and how it is taught.

This change in orientation has major practical implications for the entire curriculum process, since a negotiated curriculum cannot be introduced and managed in the same way as one which is prescribed by the teacher or teaching institutions. In particular, it places the burden for all aspects of curriculum development on the teacher.

In a curriculum based on the traditional ends–means model, a fixed series of steps is followed. Thus, in the curriculum planning process proposed by Taba (1962), planning, implementation and evaluation occur in sequential order, and most of the key decisions about aims and objectives, materials and methodology are made before there is any encounter between teacher and learner.

In fact, studies have demonstrated that most teachers simply do not operate in this way. Thus, Shavelson and Stern write:

> Most teachers are trained to plan instruction by (*a*) specifying (behavioural) objectives, (*b*) specifying students' entry behaviour, (*c*) selecting and sequencing learning activities so as to move learners from entry behaviours to objectives and (*d*) evaluating the outcomes of instruction in order to improve planning. While this prescriptive model of planning may be one of the most consistently taught features of the curriculum of teacher education programmes, the model is consistently not used in teachers' planning in schools. Obviously there is a mismatch between the demands of the classroom and the prescriptive planning model.
>
> (Shavelson and Stern 1981:477)

In this work, we shall look at what teachers do focus on in the planning, implementation and evaluation of language courses. From studies of teacher practice a negotiated curriculum model is developed in which much of the consultation, decision making and planning is informal and takes place during the course of programme delivery.

Most of the studies on which this work is based are reported here for the first time. They include a large-scale study of the teacher as curriculum planner in which over eight hundred teachers participated. Also included are smaller-scale empirical studies of teachers' involvement in content selection, methodology, materials selection and adaptation and assessment.

One of the major assumptions underlying the learner-centred philosophy is that, given the constraints that exist in most learning contexts, it is impossible to teach learners everything they need to know in class. (While this is certainly true of adult contexts, it is probably also true of other contexts as well.) What little class time there is must therefore be used as effectively as possible to teach those aspects of the language which the learners themselves deem to be most urgently required, thus increasing surrender value and consequent student motivation.

In consequence, while one major aim or set of aims will relate to the teaching of specific language skills, other aims will relate to the development of learning skills. Such aims may include the following:

– to provide learners with efficient learning strategies
– to assist learners identify their own preferred ways of learning
– to develop skills needed to negotiate the curriculum
– to encourage learners to set their own objectives
– to encourage learners to adopt realistic goals and time frames
– to develop learners' skills in self-evaluation.

The adoption of a learner-centred orientation implies differentiated curricula for different learners. This is because it is unrealistic to expect extensive participation in curriculum planning by learners with little experience of language and learning. When dealing with inexperienced learners, it is often necessary for the teacher to begin by making most of the decisions. For this reason the curriculum is conceptualised, as much by processes for carrying out curriculum tasks as by products (that is, the specification of content, lists of methodological options and so on).

1.4 The Curriculum Process

The key elements in the curriculum model proposed here are as follows: initial planning procedures (including data collection and learner grouping); content selection and gradation; methodology (which includes the selection of learning activities and materials); and ongoing monitoring, assessment and evaluation. A brief description of these elements and their functions within a learner-centred curriculum follow and are elaborated upon in the body of the text.

The first step in the curriculum process is the collection of information about learners in order to diagnose what Richterich (1972) refers to as their objective needs, that is, needs which are external to the learner. This initial data collection is usually superficial, relating mainly to factual information such as current proficiency level, age, educational background, previous learning experiences, time in the target culture and previous and current occupation. It is also sometimes possible to obtain more subjective information on preferred length and intensity of course, preferred learning arrangement, learning goals and information relating to preferred methodology, learning-style preferences and so on. However, this sort of information, relating to a learner's subjective needs as an individual in the learning situation, can often only be obtained once a course has begun.

If the information is collected before the learners are assigned to a class, it can be used for initial class placement purposes. At this point, a decision has to be made as to the weighting which will be given to the different kinds of needs which have been assessed. This will depend very much on the relative importance which is accorded by teachers to factors such as language proficiency, life-style, learning preferences and so on. In making a placement decision, these factors have to be balanced against the administrative and resource constraints under which the programme has to operate. Thus it is perfectly feasible to imagine a situation in which the same learner might well be placed in one centre in an 'intermediate class', while in another he would be placed in an 'English for motor mechanics' group and in yet another in a 'young, fast learners' category.

While language proficiency continues to be the single most important grouping criterion in most language teaching institutions, it is worth exploring other possible types of class arrangement. In developing more diverse grouping arrangements it is important for teachers to accept the notion that the grouping convention of 'twenty students of the same proficiency level for twenty hours a week' (or whatever the convention might be) is not the only arrangement, nor even the most desirable one. Unfortunately, from the evidence collected during the study reported in Chapter 10, it is often administrative inflexibility which precludes more imaginative learner groupings.

Content selection is an important component of a learner-centred curriculum. In such a curriculum clear criteria for content selection give guidance on the selection of materials and learning activities and assist in assessment and evaluation. By making explicit the content objectives of a course and, eventually, by training learners to set their own objectives, the following benefits can accrue:

Learners come to have a more realistic idea of what can be achieved in a given course.
Learning comes to be seen as the gradual accretion of achievable goals.
Students develop greater sensitivity to their role as language learners and their rather vague notions of what it is to be a learner become much sharper.
Self-evaluation becomes more feasible.
Classroom activities can be seen to relate to learners' real-life needs.
Skills development can be seen as a gradual, rather than an all-or-nothing, process.

A crucial distinction between traditional and learner-centred curriculum development is that, in the latter, no decision is binding. This is particularly true of content selection and gradation. These will need to be modified during the course of programme delivery as the learners' skills develop, their self awareness as learners grows and their perceived needs change.

It is therefore important that the content selected at the beginning of a course is not seen as definitive; it will vary, and will probably have to be modified as learners experience different kinds of learning activities and as teachers obtain more information about their subjective needs (relating to such things as affective needs, expectations and preferred learning style). It is the outcomes of ongoing dialogue between teachers and learners which will determine content and learning objectives.

The selection of content and objectives is therefore something which is shaped and refined during the initial stages of a learning arrangement rather than being completely pre-determined. This is because the most valuable learner data can usually only be obtained in an informal way after relationships have been established between teachers and learners.

The initial data collection, which is used principally for grouping learners, generally provides only fairly superficial information which can be used to make rough predictions about communicative needs. The most useful information, relating to subjective learner needs, can be obtained only once a course has begun and a relationship is established between teacher and learners. It is these subjective needs, derivable from information on learners' wants, expectations and affective needs which are of most value in selecting content and methodology.

As most learners find it difficult to articulate their needs and preferences, the initial stages of a course can be spent in providing a range of learning experiences. It is unrealistic to expect learners who have never experienced a particular approach to be able to express an opinion about it. This does not mean, however, that activities and materials should be foisted on learners at the whim of the teacher. Learners should be encouraged to reflect upon their learning experiences and articulate those they prefer, and those they feel suit them as learners.

With low-level learners, developing a critical self-awareness can best be facilitated by the use of first-language resources. In some cases the use of bilingual assistants may be a possibility. In other cases translated activity evaluation sheets should be used. These need not be elaborate. In fact they may simply require the learners to say whether or not they liked a given activity. Sample self-evaluation sheets are provided in Chapter 8.

Methodology, which includes learning activities and materials, is generally the area where there is the greatest potential for conflict between teacher and learner. In a traditional curriculum, this conflict would probably be ignored on the grounds that the 'teacher knows best'. In a learner-centred curriculum, it is crucial that any conflicts be resolved. Evidence from recent studies documenting widespread mismatches between teacher and learner expectations are examined in the chapter on methodology. The solution to methodological mismatches is to be found in techniques and procedures for negotiation and consultation. As Brindley suggests:

> Since, as we have noted, a good many learners are likely to have fixed ideas about course content, learning activities, teaching methods and so forth, it seems that teachers will continually have to face the problem of deciding to what extent to make compromises. However, if programmes are to be learner-centred, then learners' wishes should be canvassed and taken into account, even if they conflict with the wishes of the teacher. This is not to suggest that the teacher should give learners everything that they want – evidence from teachers suggests that some sort of compromise is usually possible, but only after there has been discussion concerning what both parties believe and want.

(Brindley 1984:111)

The value of negotiation and consultation between teacher and learner is vividly illustrated in the case study which forms part of Chapter 10.

Evaluation is the final component in the curriculum model. Traditionally, evaluation occurs at the final stage in the curriculum process. In the model proposed here, however, evaluation is parallel with other curriculum activities and may occur at various times during the planning and implementation phases, as well as during a specified evaluation phase. In the model, course evaluation is separated from student assessment (Shaw and Dowsett 1986).

The purpose of assessment is to determine whether or not the objectives of a course of instruction have been achieved. In the case of a failure to achieve objectives, it is the purpose of evaluation to make some determination of why this might have been so. Questions relating to evaluation include the following:

Who is to evaluate?
How are they to evaluate?
What are they to evaluate?
At what point in the curriculum process will evaluation occur?
What are the purposes of the evaluation? In other words, what will
     happen to the curriculum as a result of evaluation activities?

In traditional curriculum models, evaluation has been identified with testing and is seen as an activity which is carried out at the end of the learning process, often by someone who is not connected with the course itself. (In other words, the emphasis is on summative rather than formative evaluation.) In a learner-centred system, on the other hand, evaluation generally takes the form of an informal monitoring which is carried on alongside the teaching–learning process, principally by the participants in the process, that is, the teachers and learners.

Self-evaluation by both teachers and learners will also be promoted. By providing learners with skills in evaluating materials, learning activities and their own achievement of objectives, evaluation is built into the teaching process. By encouraging teachers to evaluate critically their own performance, evaluation becomes an integral part of both curriculum and teacher development.

Any element within the curriculum may be evaluated. At the planning stage, needs analysis techniques and procedures may be evaluated, while, during implementation, elements to be evaluated may include materials, learning activities, sequencing, learning arrangements, teacher performance and learner achievement.

With more advanced learners, it is often possible not only to train learners to identify causes of learning failure but also to suggest remedies. Such consciousness-raising activities can assist learners to monitor and evaluate their own learning processes.

1.5 The Structure of the Study

Chapter 2 looks in detail at some of the theoretical and philosophical perspectives which have been articulated in curriculum development in general, and in language teaching in particular. The various elements in the curriculum are described, and it is suggested that, until fairly recently, some of the essential elements in the curriculum have either been seriously neglected or completely overlooked. Chapter 3 looks at the background to the development of a learner-centred approach to curriculum development, with particular reference to the language curriculum. Different philosophical approaches to the curriculum are examined, and a contrast is drawn between subject-centred and learner-centred approaches. A rationale for the learner-centred approach is drawn from work on adult learning and communicative language teaching. Finally the chapter looks at the roles, functions and responsibilities of the teacher within a learner-centred curriculum.

Chapter 4 is concerned with the initial planning processes. It looks at the controversy surrounding needs analysis, discusses procedures for grouping learners and provides some practical suggestions for data collection which have been developed by teachers.

Chapter 5 considers the questions of content selection and gradation. Various principles for selecting content are discussed, and ways in which such content, once selected, may be graded are outlined.

Methodology is considered in Chapter 6. The perspective taken is that of the communicative curriculum, and it is suggested that a 'weak' interpretation of the communicative movement allows the greatest flexibility. The importance of learner consultation in selecting learning activities is also discussed. Recent research into second-language acquisition is presented, along with a study designed to demonstrate its practical implications.

Chapter 7 looks at resources. It is suggested that authenticity is a key concept in any programme designed to provide learners in class with the sorts of skills they will need to communicate effectively outside. However, a broad view of authenticity, encompassing learner response as well as textual source, is stressed. The notion of the community as a resource is also explored.

Chapters 8 and 9 address issues relating to monitoring, assessment and evaluation. In these chapters it is suggested that encouraging self-assessment on the part of learners will raise their sensitivity as language learners. It is also suggested that self-evaluation on the part of teachers, particularly through small-scale action research projects, is a valuable means of promoting professional development.

The final chapter presents the results of a large-scale ethnographic study of the difficulties faced by teachers in implementing a learner-centred curriculum model. It also draws together some of the central themes in the book, and points the way for future directions. In particular, it suggests that there is a pressing need for an empirical as well as a theoretical base for curriculum development. In order for the curriculum to be truly learner-centred, there is a need for documentation, not only of what learners want from language courses, but also of what they are capable of doing at various stages of proficiency.

1.6   Conclusion

In their analysis of theory and practice in education, MacDonald and Walker have this to say:

> Happy alliances between theorist and practitioner in our system are rare: more often, the relationship is one of mutual mistrust punctuated by open antagonism. Between sub-groups of practitioners also, and perhaps particularly between teachers and managers, the unity of common purpose rests on almost religious observance of territorial boundaries. Practitioners can, however, generally rely on each other for support when faced with an external enemy, such as public criticism, whereas the theorists' behaviour in such circumstances is less predictable.
>
> Partly as a consequence of this, education has a highly developed and long-standing mythology which acts as a protective public image projected by its members. At all levels of the system what people think they are doing, what they say they are doing, what they appear to others to be doing and what in fact they are doing, may be sources of considerable discrepancy.
>
> (MacDonald and Walker 1975:7–8)

One of the central themes of this study is that such discrepancies will continue as long as a simple equation is assumed between what is planned, what is taught and what is learned. It is only when the complex inter-relationships of the various elements within the curriculum are studied together that we might begin to get an accurate picture of what is going on. However, such a picture is only likely to emerge if a truce is called in the war between theorist and practitioner. Both must be prepared to admit that they need the other so that theory might be constantly tested against practice.

2 Curriculum Processes

2.1 Traditional Approaches to the Curriculum

Why does Teacher A teach functions but not structures? Why does Teacher B try to encourage learners to discover their own errors rather than correcting the learners herself? Why does Teacher C try to develop communication skills through role play, language games and so on, rather than through drills and controlled practice activities? Why does Teacher D create all her own materials through authentic sources, while Teacher E, who has students with similar needs, uses coursebooks written by someone else?

Some teachers claim that teaching is essentially a practical activity, and has very little to do with the theoretical deliberations of educational philosophers, psychologists and curriculum designers. Stern, in fact, suggests that this is a characteristic of language teachers in general:

> Language teachers can be said to regard themselves as practical people and not as theorists. Some might even say they are opposed to 'theory', expressing their opposition in such remarks as 'It's all very well in theory, but it won't work in practice'.
>
> (Stern 1983:23)

However, as Stern goes on to observe, implicit in all the decisions made by the teacher relating to classroom practice, materials, methodology and content is a theory about the nature of language and the nature of language learning. Not all teachers will be able to articulate their theories, but they will have them just the same, and they lie behind the sorts of questions posed at the beginning of this chapter.

Curriculum planning can be seen as the systematic attempt by educationalists and teachers to specify and study planned intervention into the educational enterprise. In this chapter we shall explore some of the central concepts behind the study of the curriculum and look at a number of different models which have been developed to specify and assist in the planning, presentation and evaluation of learning.

One way of looking at the curriculum is to see it as an attempt to specify what should happen in the classroom, to describe what actually does happen, and to attempt to reconcile the differences between what 'should be' and what actually 'is'.

Lawton (1973) sees the gap between theory and practice, that is, the gap between what should be and what is, as one of the central problems of the curriculum. He suggests that:

> This gap exists at a number of levels; for example, the difference between what teachers suggest should happen and what can be observed in the classroom, the gap between educational theory as taught in colleges and universities and the 'common-sense' practical approach of teachers in schools. Students leaving college and entering schools are sometimes advised by practising teachers to 'forget all that theory and get on with the real teaching'. But every teacher is involved in decisions of a theoretical nature: if he decides to teach mathematics but forbid playing cards in class, he is basing his decision on some kind of theory of what is worthwhile; if he decides that a book is too difficult for a certain class or pupil, he is making use of psychological theories about intelligence, or ability, or stages of development.
>
> (Lawton 1973:7–8)

One of the most influential curriculum developers this century is Tyler, whose best known work, *Basic Principles of Curriculum and Instruction*, was published in 1949. For many, this book is seen as the early bible of curriculum design. In it, Tyler provides a model for the systematic development of the curriculum. He asserts that the development of any curriculum for any subject whatsoever must be based on a consideration of four fundamental questions. These are as follows:

What educational purposes should the school seek to attain?
What educational experiences can be provided that are likely to attain these purposes?
How can these educational experiences be effectively organised?
How can we determine whether these purposes are being attained?

The first question forces the curriculum developer to contemplate and clarify the nature of the educational enterprise in which he or she is involved. In other words, it requires the specification of aims, goals and objectives. The second question relates to the content of instruction and requires the curriculum designer to articulate the subject matter which will be used as a vehicle for attaining the pre-specified aims, goals and objectives. The third question, relating to the organisation of the educational experiences, requires the curriculum designer to articulate the principles for staging and sequencing input for the curriculum. The final question, on attainment of pre-specified purposes or objectives, relates to the area of evaluation.

While the model articulated by Tyler has been extremely influential in educational circles, it has by no means been free from criticism. One of the major criticisms is that it is the archetypal 'ballistic' model, suggesting as it does that curriculum activity occurs in a series of discrete and sequential stages. In the first instance aims and objectives are specified; content is then selected and organised, and finally, after the teaching has been completed, there is an evaluation phase to determine whether the aims and objectives have been achieved.

The other major criticism of the model is that it represents an ends–means view of education. Lawton suggests that:

> One objection to the whole curriculum model based on the four-stage progression from objectives to content to organisation to evaluation is that this is far too simple. For one reason, it is open to Bruner's suggestion that leaving evaluation until the final stage of the curriculum process is rather like doing military intelligence after the war is over: in other words, evaluation should take place at every stage. This would make the curriculum model a cyclical one rather than a linear model.
>
> (*op cit.*:14)

It was criticism of linear models of curriculum development which led Wheeler (1967) to develop a more integrated model. This has similar elements to Tyler's in that it begins with aims, goals and objectives, goes on to the selection of learning experiences and thence to the selection of content, takes into consideration the organisation and integration of learning experiences and then specifies evaluation. However, it differs from Tyler's model in that it allows for recycling, so that evaluation feeds back into aims, goals and objectives. In this way the evaluation stage provides a basis for modifying the aims, goals and objectives the next time a course or module is taught.

By the end of the 1960s, thinking on the curriculum had become much more sophisticated. This can be seen in Kerr's (1968) interactive curriculum model, which has four major interactive elements: objectives, evaluation, knowledge and school learning experiences, each of which has subsidiary elements. All of these elements interact in the learning–teaching situation, and a change in one element in the model leads to changes in all other elements.

An influential figure in the curriculum field was Stenhouse, whose major publication, *An Introduction to Curriculum Research and Development*, was published in 1975. The fact that many of the ideas he advanced are only now gaining widespread recognition indicates that he was well in advance of his time. With curriculum specialists such as Stenhouse, however, it is important to bear in mind the social, political and educational contexts in which they worked.

Some language specialists have recently adopted Stenhouse's 'process' curriculum. While process models may represent a paradigm-shift in language curriculum development, it should be remembered that Stenhouse's model was developed within the context of his strong commitment to a subject-centred view of the curriculum, and may not necessarily be as relevant in systems subscribing to other philosophies or approaches.

Stenhouse defines the curriculum as:

> An attempt to communicate the essential principles and features of an educational proposal in such a form that it is open to critical scrutiny and capable of effective translation into practice.
>
> (Stenhouse 1975:4)

He suggests that a curriculum should consist of three major parts relating to planning, empirical study and justification. Each of these consists of subsidiary parts as set out in the following table.

TABLE 2.1 MAJOR ELEMENTS IN A GENERALISED CURRICULUM MODEL

A. Planning consists of:

1 Principles for the selection of content — what is to be learned and taught
2 Principles for the development of a teaching strategy — how it is to be learned and taught
3 Principles for the making of decisions about sequence
4 Principles on which to diagnose the strengths and weakness of individual students and differentiate the general principles 1, 2 and 3 above to meet individual cases

B. In empirical study:

1 Principles on which to study and evaluate the progress of students
2 Principles on which to study and evaluate the progress of teachers
3 Guidance as to the feasibility of implementing the curriculum in varying school contexts, pupil contexts, environments and peer group situations
4 Information about the variability of effects in differing contexts and on different pupils and an understanding of the causes of the variation

C. In relation to justification:

A formulation of the aim or intention of the curriculum which is accessible to critical scrutiny.

The process model developed by Stenhouse has three particularly useful things to say about curriculum development in general. In the first place, it accords a central place in the curriculum process to an analysis of what is actually happening, in contrast with the pious statements that are often made about what ought to be happening. It is thus centred on the implemented rather than the planned curriculum (Bartlett and Butler 1985). Secondly, it recognises the central role played by the teacher in the curriculum development process. Finally, it gives recognition to the fact that effective curriculum development is largely a matter of effective teacher development by suggesting that curriculum change will only find its way into the classroom if teachers themselves become the principal agents of curriculum change through critical analysis and reflection on their current performance. Stenhouse's ideas have been taken up and developed by curriculum theorists such as Kemmis and McTaggart (1982), who have proposed an action-research orientation to curriculum development. Their use of action research in the language classroom is discussed in Chapter 9.

At this point, mention should be made of the distinction between the terms 'curriculum' and 'syllabus'. In the United States, it is customary to use the term 'curriculum', rather than 'syllabus', to refer to all aspects of the planning, implementation and evaluation of curriculum. The term is also used for a particular course of instruction. In Britain, the term 'syllabus' is used to denote that part of curriculum activity concerned with the specification and ordering of course content or input. In other words, it is concerned with the 'what' of the curriculum. In this book, the term 'curriculum' incorporates those elements designated by the term 'syllabus' along with considerations of methodology and evaluation. In relation to language teaching, the key elements for consideration within the curriculum are as follows: initial planning including needs analysis, grouping learners, goal and objective setting, selection and grading of content, methodology (which includes materials and learning activities), learning arrangements (incorporating learning modes and environments), and finally assessment and evaluation.

In this section we have taken a fairly general look at the concept of the curriculum. We have looked at the evolution of the curriculum from the 'ballistic', ends–means model of Tyler, through to the process model articulated by Stenhouse. We have seen that the aim of curriculum theory is to provide a more systematic approach to education. Unfortunately, the systematic consideration of the curriculum has been left to 'experts', and it has only been in recent years that the central role of the teacher as curriculum developer has been recognised. In the next section we shall look at curriculum planning within ESL, and trace the application of some of the ideas outlined in this section to the field of language teaching. In the final section we shall consider the implications of the learner-centred philosophy for systematic curriculum development.

2.2 ESL and Curriculum Planning

Until recently, there has been a comparative neglect of curriculum theorising in relation to ESL. This neglect could well be due to the dominance (and, some would say, the disproportionate influence) of theoretical linguistics over language teaching. Language learning has been seen as a linguistic, rather than an educational, matter, and there has been a tendency to overlook research and development as well as planning processes related to general educational principles in favour of linguistic principles and, in recent years, second language acquisition research. Thus, decisions on selecting and grading input have traditionally been made on linguistic grounds. Recent empirical research into learnability and speech processing constraints has demonstrated that there is not always a direct correlation between linguistic predictions of difficulty and what learners actually do find difficult, and only recently has attention focused on the selection and grading of input on the basis of what is actually learnable at any given stage (Johnston 1985). As mentioned in Chapter 1, recent researchers have tended to take a broader view.

Clark (1985a), borrowing from a framework developed by Skilbeck, relates developments in language teaching to a number of dominant mainstream educational ideologies. These are Classical Humanism, Reconstructionism and Progressivism. Before looking at Clark's analysis, it might be worth looking at the way he conceptualises 'curriculum renewal' (a term he favours over the more widely used curriculum 'development').

Clark suggests that:

> ... this takes in the creation of syllabuses in which educational, subject-specific and learner-orientated objectives (content and methodology) are reconciled, the creation of resources to provide learning experiences for the learner, the writing of principles and guidelines to assist teachers to tailor their classroom practices to the requirements of their learners, the elaboration of an assessment scheme to monitor and measure pupil progress, the devising of strategies to evaluate the curriculum itself, and last but not least, the working out of strategies for teacher development, so that teachers are enabled to renew their own curriculum in the light of their own classroom reality.
>
> (Clark 1985a:3)

Within this broad concept of the curriculum, Clark suggests that the key elements are objectives, content and methodology. In any curriculum design, certain ends will have to be reached through the specification of content and methodology. In Clark's mind, the key problems to be solved in curriculum design are: first, whether ends should be predetermined, or whether they should be the result of an open-ended learning process;

whether content should be selected to meet predetermined ends or whether it should be selected on its inherent merits; and finally, how conflicting views about learning can be translated into effective methodology.

Clark attributes many of the problems currently besetting language teaching to a failure on the part of language teachers to take a broader perspective. He says that:

> Much unnecessary confusion has been created by those who have thought the solution to the language curriculum problem could be found in one part of the jigsaw to the exclusion of other parts. Thus, panaceas have been sought in methodology alone, or in catch-all technological aids ... or in 'graded tests', as if assessment by itself could improve the teaching–learning process, or in the production of new teaching materials, or in the elaboration of ever more complex syllabuses such as the various Threshold documents, or in studies of acquisition of language development, or in impressionistic global descriptions of proficiency at different levels.
>
> (*op cit.*:6)

Classical humanism is the educational philosophy underpinning the subject-centred view of learning. It is the view which has been most savagely attacked by the radical sociologists of education. In language teaching, it can be seen to underpin the views of those who believe that curriculum planning should start with an analysis of the target language, rather than with the needs of the learners (see for example Young 1971).

According to Clark, reconstructionism is the philosophy underpinning the ends–means, or objectives, approach to curriculum design. This is the model which was first articulated by Tyler, and later sophisticated by people such as Taba (1962). The ends–means model, according to Clark, is the philosophical driving force behind much of the work of the Council of Europe. Clark documents a number of criticisms of this approach, suggesting, in particular, that it reduces the teacher to the role of a mere implementor of someone else's curriculum. It has also been suggested that the formulation of objectives, on which the model itself rests, is defective in that while certain communicative objectives relating to skills such as the use of transactional language are easy to operationalise, it is much more difficult to produce objectives for the expressive and creative functions of language. In raising this particular objection, Clark cites Stenhouse, who asserts that it is the unpredictable rather than the predictable outcomes of student behaviour which make education worthwhile.

The major objection to the ends–means model seems to be that it concentrates exclusively on the products rather than the processes of learning, and assumes that specifying the end points of learning is all that the curriculum designer needs to do. However, there is growing recognition within the profession that specification of the end products (the syllabus design component of the curriculum) must also be accompanied by specifications of methodology (that is indications on how to reach that end point).

Progressivism, the third educational ideology, finds expression in the process syllabus. Proponents of the process approach are Breen and Candlin (1980), Prabhu (1983), Long (1985) and Long and Crookes (1986). Process curricula are less concerned with specifying content or output than with the sorts of learning activities in which learners should engage. They therefore align themselves more with methodology than with syllabus design. In such curricula, specification is more in terms of tasks and problems for the learner to grapple with than in terms of linguistic items (whether these be structures, notions or functions).

One of the most widely-reported experiments in the use of process curricula, is Prabhu's Bangalore project. The language program in this project is described in the following terms:

> The program is constructed around a series of problems, requiring the use of English, which have to be solved by the learner. The problems are introduced as specific tasks in which the students have to interpret the language data – for example the timetable or set of rules or a map with its rubric – and use the data for particular purposes. Tasks are usually preceded by pre-tasks, in which the teacher performs a task similar to the one the students will be asked to perform themselves, in interaction with the class, using whatever language that seems appropriate for this purpose. Thus the level of language used by the teacher is determined by the demands of the problem, and by the teacher's natural powers of simplification, unplanned and spontaneously structured.
>
> (Brumfit 1984:104)

Clark's analysis shows that while language teaching may have escaped the educational mainstream it has been inevitably influenced by trends, developments and philosophies within that mainstream. Recent writings by Richards (1984), and Nunan (1985a), indicate that applied linguists are beginning to recognise the need to set language teaching within a broader educational context. It is to the models developed by these two writers that we now turn.

Richards (1984) begins his survey of the field by pointing to the narrow conception of curriculum development that exists within language teaching, where the focus has been almost exclusively on language syllabuses, that is, on the specification of content and input, to the exclusion of other crucially important aspects of the curriculum development process such as needs analysis, methodology and evaluation. He attempts to redress this by presenting a curriculum model in which language teaching is seen as a set of processes and procedures which are both systematic and interrelated.

The essential elements in the model are needs analysis, objective setting, content and methodology, and evaluation. The raw material from which the curriculum developer creates language courses includes information about the target language, information about learners, information about the delivery system, a learning theory, a teaching theory, assessment and evaluation procedures. Underlying the model is Taba's (1962) model of curriculum processes, and it can therefore be seen to reside within the ends–means tradition. This is not to say that the model is necessarily dated. In fact, Richards incorporates into his model a proficiency-oriented view of language and language use, a view which is consistent with an ends–means approach.

By suggesting that the starting point for curriculum development be an analysis of learner needs rather than a linguistic analysis, Richards has distanced himself from the linguistic tradition in language teaching course design. He suggests that needs analysis allows for greater numbers of people to be involved in curriculum development, it also enables goals and objectives to be identified, and provides data for evaluation and accountability.

Richards sees the specification of objectives as crucial in curriculum processes predicated on a proficiency-oriented view of language. He states that:

> Proficiency, however described, refers to a product or result of successful language acquisition, and since it represents a very general concept, needs to be operationalised in making decisions about content and procedure in teaching. This is done through the development of program goals or objectives. In language teaching a number of different ways of stating objectives are commonly employed, variations in practice reflecting different perceptions of the nature of second- or foreign-language proficiency. Current approaches include behavioural, process, content and proficiency based objectives.
>
> (Richards 1984:10)

In considering content and methodology, Richards suggests that there are two different orientations that the curriculum designer can take. The first of these is to look at language input specification as the fundamental basis for methodology. The other is to focus on instructional processes and not bother with an explicit specification of language content. The content-oriented approach has dominated language syllabus design for many years, first in the guise of structural and latterly in the guise of functional–notional syllabuses. Process-oriented alternatives include the 'fringe' methodologies such as Silent Way, Community Language Learning and Suggestopedia. It also includes task-based, and process-based syllabuses such as the Bangalore syllabus of Prabhu. In discussing methodology, Richards suggests that regardless of orientation there are three underlying components. These are (a) a linguistic dimension which justifies what aspects of language will be taught, (b) a psycholinguistic dimension which includes an account of the processes underlying learning, and (c) a teaching dimension, which relates to learning experience activities and tasks and to the role of teachers learners and materials in the learning system.

Richards comments on the general lack of evaluation procedures in language teaching, attributing this to the relatively short life span of most teaching methods and also to the absence of the sort of systematic approach to curriculum development that he is advocating. He suggests that the purpose of evaluation is to determine whether the objectives of a programme have been attained and, where they have not been attained, to suggest procedures for improvement. He describes a comprehensive evaluation model taken from Omaggio *et al.* (1979) which contains eight steps. These are as follows:

1. Identify a set of programme goals and objectives to be evaluated.
2. Identify programme factors relevant to the attainment of these objectives.
3. For each factor in Step 2, develop a set of criteria that would indicate that the objectives are being successfully attained.
4. Design appropriate instruments to assess each factor according to the criteria outlined.
5. Collect the data that is needed.
6. Compare data with desired results.
7. Match your discrepancy.
8. Prepare an evaluation report.

The course design model developed by Nunan (1985a) is similar in many respects to that devised by Richards. The essential elements in this model include needs analysis, goal identification, objective setting, materials development, learning activities, learning mode and environment and evaluation. The model differs from that proposed by Richards, however, in that apart, from initial *ad hoc* needs analysis for the purposes of grouping learners, curriculum development activities occur during the process of teaching and learning. The curriculum development process is cyclical and is thus similar to that developed by Wheeler (1967). It is also interactive, recognising that the impetus for curriculum development can begin with any of the elements in the model and that a change in one element will affect other elements. For example, the discovery of new materials may suggest a modification to objectives, learning arrangements and evaluation. Use of new materials will almost certainly have an effect on methodology and the sorts of learning activities which take place in the classroom.

The other aspect of the model which differs slightly from previous ones is the prominence it gives to the teacher in the course design process. Reassessment of the role of the teacher in curriculum development is a major preoccupation of the present work and is expanded upon in the pages which follow.

In this section we have looked at recent language curriculum development models. We have seen that until fairly recently there has been a lack of balance in the attention devoted to different elements within the model with the focus being either exclusively on the selection and grading of content, or on methodology.

The current need is for language curriculum designers to look beyond linguistics to the general field of educational research and theory for assistance in developing curricula. There is also a need for curriculum development to be systematic, and for due consideration to be given to all the key elements in the curriculum development process.

2.3   Summary

The curriculum model developed in the rest of this book is a synthesis of the product-oriented ends–means model, and the process-oriented approach first proposed for language teaching by applied linguists such as Breen and Candlin. One of the articles of faith underpinning this book is that any curriculum which fails to give due consideration to both process and product will be defective. Thus, while the model contains procedures for developing goals and objectives, and for evaluating these, it sees the various curriculum development activities as ongoing processes within the teaching–learning process. Important in planning, presenting and evaluating learning outcomes will be joint consultation and negotiation between teachers and learners. Adopting a process orientation allows for greater flow and integration between planning processes, implementation processes and evaluation. The model thus rejects the ballistic nature of ends–means models where planning occurs before course delivery and evaluation after course delivery. It also rejects the general tendency for some ends–means approaches to downplay the role of methodology or ignore it completely.

3 Learner-Centred Curriculum Development

3.1 Introduction

One way of typifying curriculum models is in the degree to which they allow curriculum development to occur at the local level. A fully centralised curriculum, as the name suggests, is one which is devised in a centralised location and then disseminated (this is sometimes known as the centre-periphery model for obvious reasons). Many school curricula developed during the 1950s and 1960s accorded with this centralised model. They were often produced by a government department or agency, and then disseminated to a wide range of learning institutions. The responsibility of the teacher in such systems was often little more than to implement the curriculum and to act as 'classroom manager'. An example of a centralised approach to language teaching is the *Situational English* course which was developed for teaching ESL in Australia during the 1960s and early 1970s. During this time, it was possible to go into language classrooms all over the country and find a similar curriculum in place for teaching a wide range of learners. In those days the only criteria for differentiating learners was level of proficiency.

During the 1960s, the relative inflexibility of centralised curricula, and a change in educational thinking which paid more attention to the learner, led to the 'school-based' curriculum development movement. School-based curricula are devised either wholly or in part within the teaching institution itself. Such curricula are capable of being much more responsive than centralised curricula to the needs and interests of the learners they serve. The learner-centred movement in ESL/EFL is partly an offspring of the school-based curriculum movement.

A perennial tension in language teaching is between those who subscribe to a subject-centred view and those who subscribe to a learner-centred view of language and language learning. The subject-centred view sees learning a language as essentially the mastering of a body of knowledge. The learner-centred view, on the other hand, tends to view language acquisition as a process of acquiring skills rather than a body of knowledge. Both viewpoints are quite valid, and most courses will reflect elements of both. It is the relative emphasis given to language as a body of content to be internalised, or language as communicative processes to be developed, which will determine which of the labels 'subject-centred' or 'learner-centred' should apply to a given curriculum proposal.

Proponents of learner-centred curricula are less interested in learners acquiring the totality of the language than in assisting them gain the communicative and linguistic skills they need to carry out real-world tasks. Implicit in this learner-centred view is a recognition that no one person (not even a native speaker) ever masters every aspect of the language. If it were possible to master every aspect of every skill in a given language, and if one had unlimited time to teach or learn another language, then there would be no need to make choices, and consequently no debate. However, given the fact that most learners do not have unlimited time (many may have only between 150–300 hours of formal instruction) it is crucial that appropriate choices be made.

3.2   Theoretical Bases for Learner-Centred Curricula

In this section the theoretical background to the development of learner-centred language teaching is explored. We shall take a brief look at the theory and practice of adult learning before looking at the development of communicative language learning and teaching. The proficiency movement is also described. Finally we shall look at the implications of the learner-centred philosophy for the language teacher. This provides the context for an examination of the nature of the curriculum, and the various elements within a curriculum model which come into prominence when the curriculum is seen from a learner-centred perspective.

The theory and practice of adult learning or androgogy has had a long history. However, it is only comparatively recently that this theory and practice has been related to adult language learning. The most prominent theorist in the field of adult learning is Knowles (1983), whose book *The Adult Learner: A Neglected Species* became very influential in adult learning circles.

Two other specialists in adult learning theory whose work has been influential in language teaching circles are Brundage and MacKeracher (1980). Their book *Adult Learning Principles and Their Application to Programme Planning* is regularly cited these days in the language teaching literature. Some of the principles of adult learning identified by Brundage and MacKeracher are as follows:

> Adults who value their own experience as a resource for further learning or whose experience is valued by others are better learners.
> Adults learn best when they are involved in developing learning objectives for themselves which are congruent with their current and idealised self concept.
> Adults have already developed organised ways of focusing on, taking

in and processing information. These are referred to as cognitive style.

The learner reacts to all experience as he perceives it, not as the teacher presents it.

Adults enter into learning activities with an organised set of descriptions and feelings about themselves which influence the learning process.

Adults are more concerned with whether they are changing in the direction of their own idealised self-concept than whether they are meeting standards and objectives set for them by others.

Adults do not learn when over-stimulated or when experiencing extreme stress or anxiety.

Those adults who can process information through multiple channels and have learnt 'how to learn' are the most productive learners.

Adults learn best when the content is personally relevant to past experience or present concerns and the learning process is relevant to life experiences.

Adults learn best when novel information is presented through a variety of sensory modes and experiences, with sufficient repetitions and variations on themes to allow distinctions in patterns to emerge.

(Brundage and MacKeracher 1980:21–31)

The research surveyed by Brundage and MacKeracher in formulating their principles of adult learning indicate that adult learners are profoundly influenced by past learning experiences, present concerns and future prospects. They are less interested in learning for learning's sake than in learning to achieve some immediate or not too far distant life goals. Translated to the field of language teaching, this suggests that a learner-centred rather than subject-centred approach is more likely to be consonant with the principles of adult learning. Adult learners are less likely to be interested in subscribing to the 'banking principle', that is in gaining mastery over subject matter or skills which may be useful at some far distant date, than in acquiring skills which can be put to immediate use. However, the empirical evidence on this matter is rather thin. What evidence we do have seems to suggest that adult learners vary markedly in their attitudes towards learning, their preferred learning styles and their perceptions of what is of value and what is not (Willing 1985).

In his study of adult language learners, Brindley suggests that:

> ... one of the fundamental principles underlying the notion of permanent education is that education should develop in individuals the capacity to control their own destiny and that, therefore, the learner should be seen as being at the centre of the educational process. For the teaching institution and the teacher, this means that instructional programmes should be centred around learners' needs and that learners themselves should exercise their own

> responsibility in the choice of learning objectives, content and
> methods as well as in determining the means used to assess their
> performance.
> (Brindley 1984:15)

From his survey of the literature, Brindley concludes that adult learners
are not merely passive recipients of subject matter devised by some
educational authority, but have 'a wide experience of life which can be
brought to bear in the learning process'. It is this belief among others
which leads him to adopt a learner- rather than a subject-centred
approach to the development of language curricula.

An important figure on the curriculum landscape is Munby (1978).
The Munby model, which was at first thought to hold great promise for
language syllabus design, has come increasingly under criticism in the
last few years and is now generally regarded as the core document in
the narrow-band approach to needs-based course design. This narrow-
band approach sees course design largely in terms of the specification
of the 'what' of language teaching to the exclusion of the 'how'. The
somewhat mechanical nature of the procedures for deriving course input
and the atomistic approach to language specification and learning has
been criticised as well. In fact, in some ways the Munby model can be
seen to be antithetical to the learner-centred philosophy from which it
was supposedly derived. Being based on data about the learner, rather
than incorporating data from the learner, it could be argued that the
model is only superficially learner-centred.

While the Munby model might be quite adequate for providing objective information for content specification, it fails to provide the sort of
subjective information which is at the heart of the learner-centred procedures for curriculum design. The distinction between subjective and
objective needs analysis, and procedures for using both types of analysis
in designing language curricula are considered in greater detail in Chapter
4.

3.3   Communicative Language Teaching and Learner-Centred Curricula

A major impetus to the develop of learner-centred language teaching
came with the advent of communicative language teaching. In fact, this
is more a cluster of approaches than a single methodology, which grew
out of the dissatisfaction with structuralism and the situational methods
of the 1960s. Its status was enhanced by the Council of Europe, and
some seminal documents on communicative language teaching have in
fact stemmed from this body. Prominent among these are *Threshold*

Level English by van Ek and Alexander (1980), and *Notional Syllabuses* by Wilkins (1976).

A great deal has been written in the last few years about the theory and practice of communicative language teaching. However, a basic principle underlying all communicative approaches is that learners must learn not only to make grammatically correct, propositional statements about the experiential world, but must also develop the ability to use language to get things done. These two aspects of language are captured in the distinction between the propositional and illocutionary (or functional) levels of language (Widdowson 1978). It was recognised that simply being able to create grammatically correct structures in language did not necessarily enable the learner to use the language to carry out various real-world tasks. While the learners have to be able to construct grammatically correct structures (or reasonable approximations of target language structures), they also have to do much more. In working out what this 'much more' entails, linguists and sociolinguists began to explore the concept of the speech situation. In so doing they were able to articulate some of the ways in which language is likely be influenced by situational variables. Among the more important of these variables are the situation itself, the topic of conversation, the conversational purpose, and, probably the most important of all, the relationship between interlocutors in an interaction. All of these interact in complex ways in communicative interaction.

As already indicated, early support for communicative language teaching came from the Council of Europe. Basically, the Council of Europe wanted to specify the sorts of things that language users might want to do with languages used within the European Community. Consequently, they were thinking of a specified group of adult learners using the languages of Europe to carry out specified tasks which included not only economic and business activities, but also recreational and tourist activities. It is important to be aware of this historical background because communicative approaches are currently used in many different contexts and situations, not all of which were intended by the original working party of the Council of Europe, and in consequence some Council of Europe perspectives may not be relevant.

According to Howatt, there is a strong and a weak version of communicative language teaching. He says:

> The weak version which has become more or less standard practice in the last ten years, stresses the importance of providing learners with opportunities to use their English for communicative purposes and, characteristically, attempts to integrate such activities into a wider programme of language teaching.

(Howatt 1984:279)

The strong version of communicative language teaching, however, sees language ability as being developed through activities which actually simulate target performance. In other words, class time should be spent not on language drills or controlled practice leading towards communicative language use, but in activities which require learners to do in class what they will have to do outside.

In recent years it is the weak version which seems to have gained sway. Thus, we see teachers who adhere to a communicative view of language teaching also incorporating elements of structural practice and grammar teaching into their classes. Littlewood is a proponent of the weak view of communicative language teaching. He says:

> The structural view of language has not been in any way superseded by the functional view. However, it is not sufficient on its own to account for how language is used as a means of communication. Let us take as an example a straightforward sentence such as 'Why don't you close the door?' From a structural viewpoint, it is unambiguously an interrogative. Different grammars may describe it in different ways, but none could argue that its grammatical form is that of a declarative or imperative. From a functional viewpoint, however, it is ambiguous. In different circumstances it may appear to function as a question – for example, the speaker may genuinely wish to know why his companion never closes a certain door. In others, it may function as a command . . .
>
> (Littlewood 1981:1)

In fact this weak version has so successfully synthesised traditional and 'communicative' principles that it is debatable whether the term 'communicative' is still useful. (Few teachers these days would admit to teaching 'non-communicatively'.)

In a useful survey of communicative language teaching, Quinn suggests that communicative approaches can be distinguished from traditional approaches to language pedagogy in a number of ways. These are set out in Table 3.1:

TABLE 3.1   CHARACTERISTICS OF TRADITIONAL AND COMMUNICATIVE APPROACHES

Traditional approaches	*Communicative approaches*
1 *Focus in learning*:	
Focus is on the language as a structured system of grammatical patterns.	Focus is on communication.

Traditional approaches	Communicative approaches
2 How language items are selected:	
This is done on linguistic criteria alone.	This is done on the basis of what language items the learner needs to know in order to get things done.
3 How language items are sequenced:	
This is determined on linguistic grounds.	This is determined on other grounds, with the emphasis on content, meaning and interest.
4 Degree of coverage:	
The aim is to cover the 'whole picture' of language structure by systematic linear progression.	The aim is to cover, in any particular phase, only what the learner needs and sees as important.
5 View of language:	
A language is seen as a unified entity with fixed grammatical patterns and a core of basic words.	The variety of language is accepted, and seen as determined by the character of particular communicative contexts.
6 Type of language used:	
Tends to be formal and bookish.	Genuine everyday language is emphasised.
7 What is regarded as a criterion of success:	
Aim is to have students produce formally correct sentences.	Aim is to have students communicate effectively and in a manner appropriate to the context they are working in.
8 Which language skills are emphasised:	
Reading and writing.	Spoken interactions are regarded as at least as important as reading and writing.

⟫→

Traditional approaches	Communicative approaches

9 Teacher/Student roles:

Tends to be teacher-centred.

Is student-centred.

10 Attitude to errors:

Incorrect utterances are seen as deviations from the norms of standard grammar.

Partially correct and incomplete utterances are seen as such rather than just 'wrong'.

11 Similarity/dissimilarity to natural language learning:

Reverses the natural language learning process by concentrating on the form of utterances rather than on the content.

Resembles the natural language learning process in that the content of the utterance is emphasised rather than the form.

(*Adapted from:* Quinn 1984:61–64)

3.4 Communicative Language Teaching – The Teacher's Perspective

In this section, a study is reported which investigated the attitudes of teachers towards communicative language teaching. The point of departure for the study was an earlier investigation into the methodological practices of foreign language teachers by Swaffar, Arens and Morgan (1982).

Background

The study undertaken by Swaffar, Arens and Morgan was designed to test the salience for foreign language teachers of the distinction between rationalist and empiricist approaches to language learning. Results indicated that the methodological debate which had assumed great prominence during the 1960s and 1970s and which resulted in a number of large-scale though inconclusive studies may have been based on false assumptions about the salience of different methodological practices for classroom teachers. Swaffar *et al.* concluded from their investigation that:

> Methodological labels assigned to teaching activities are, in themselves, not informative, because they refer to a pool of classroom practices which are universally used.
>
> (Swaffar, Arens and Morgan 1982:31)

Given the prominence of communicative language teaching in the literature, a study was designed to investigate the salience of 'communicative' as opposed to 'traditional' practices for second language teachers.

The Study

Following Quinn (1984) a survey instrument was constructed which consisted of statements typifying either 'traditional' or 'communicative' practices. There were also two buffer questions. Teachers were asked to rate each statement according to a five point scale. (This was adapted from the Swaffar *et al.* (1982) study.) The instrument is reproduced below.

Subjects for the study were 60 full-time and part-time teachers with the Australian Adult Migrant Education Program (AMEP). As we shall be looking at several studies of AMEP teachers in this work, it might be as well to make a short digression to describe the context in which the teachers work.

The AMEP is one of the largest single-language programmes in the world, with annual enrolments in excess of 120,000, and over 1,500 teachers. Learning arrangements and course types vary greatly, from full-time intensive to part-time courses. Programme delivery occurs through face-to-face teaching, self-access and individualised learning centres, a distance education programme and a home tutor scheme. The AMEP receives its funding and policy direction from the Australian Government Department of Immigration and Ethnic Affairs, while the administration and delivery of courses is managed by eight State and Territory educational bodies.

While all those taking part in the survey described below were concerned with the teaching of English to adult immigrants, they came from all parts of the Program and had a wide range of experience. The teachers were asked to complete the questionnaire in Table 3.2 during the course of an in-service workshop. The workshop was not concerned with communicative methodology, so the subjects were not 'primed' to respond to the items on the questionnaire in a particular way.

》→

TABLE 3.2 SURVEY QUESTIONNAIRE ON 'TRADITIONAL' AND 'COMMUNICATIVE' ACTIVITIES

Instructions:

Please rate each of the statements according to the following key:

1 Virtual non-use. This principle or activity forms little or no part of my teaching methodology.
2 Trivial incidental use. This principle or activity forms a limited part of what I do, but I tend to reject its use more than I favour its use. Somewhat disagree with use.
3 Neutral.
4 Important supplementary use. This principle forms an important supplementary part of my teaching. Somewhat agree with use.
5 Essential use. This is essential to what I do, and it forms an essential part of my practice. Use or agree with use.

1 Drills involving manipulation of formal aspects of the language system are used. ....

2 The development of fluency is more important than formal accuracy. ....

3 Activities focus on whole-task rather than part-skill practice. ....

4 Comprehension activities precede activities requiring production. ....

5 'Grammar' is explicitly taught. ....

6 Learner errors are corrected. ....

7 Activities are selected because they are interesting/enjoyable rather than because they relate to course objectives. ....

8 Activities are derived in consultation with the learner. ....

9 Activities are developed which require the learner to simulate, in class, behaviours needed to communicate outside class. ....

Comments:

Results

Each item in the survey form was rated according to the mean score, and an appropriate designation given. Ratings and item type are indicated in Table 3.3:

TABLE 3.3 RATINGS FOR ITEMS ACCORDING TO MEAN SCORE

Item	Type	Rating
1	Traditional	Trivial, incidental use
2	Communicative	Essential use
3	Communicative	Important supplementary use
4	Communicative	Important supplementary use
5	Traditional	Trivial, incidental use
6	Traditional	Trivial, incidental use
7	Buffer	Trivial, incidental use
8	Buffer	Important supplementary use
9	Communicative	Essential use

Discussion

The results demonstrate quite clearly that, for the group of teachers surveyed, the concept of 'communicative language teaching' is salient, with the three non-communicative and one of the buffer statements being accorded 'trivial incidental use'. While these results might, on the surface, appear to conflict with that obtained by Swaffar *et al.*, it is important not to read too much into them. In the first place, the study was designed to determine only what teachers said they did. It should not be assumed that their actual classroom practice followed these principles. (While this comment might seem to imply dishonesty or lack of awareness on the part of teachers, there is evidence that teachers do not, in fact, always do what they say or think they do. This evidence, which has implications for teacher development, is presented in Chapter 9.)

Another point which needs to be made and which could call into question the results is the fact that many of the teachers who commented on the survey criticised the use of questionnaires for data-collection purposes. Most of them wanted to qualify their responses in some way. a significant number stated that the response they gave would depend upon, and could vary according to, the type of students they had. Disquiet at the use of questionnaires for data-collection purposes was also expressed in other studies reported here, including the major study which forms the basis of the final chapter. It seems that, in general, teachers are loathe to give unequivocal responses on matters relating to professional practice.

The buffer statement which rated well (8) relates to the learner-centred view of involving learners in selecting activities.

In developing a learner-centred philosophy for the AMEP Ingram stated that:

> Rather than being an arbitrary academic exercise, the course followed should be responsive to the learner's needs emanating from his stage of language development and his personal interests and aspirations. Thence, it must capitalise on the learner's natural and acquired learning strategies and ensure, through community involvement, that any bridge between the learner and the Australian community is bridged and any sense of undesirable alienisation is reduced.
>
> (Ingram 1981:4)

More recently Brindley (1984) has built on the work of Ingram and others. After surveying the literature, he provides a blueprint and a framework for introducing learner-centred principles into adult ESL. The strength of Brindley's work is that it brings together theory and practice. This work is analysed in Chapter 4, and many of the practical suggestions incorporated into that chapter owe a considerable debt to Brindley.

3.5   The Concept of Language Proficiency

It is generally considered desirable for language curricula to contain explicit statements about the nature of language and language learning. While some assumptions about these concepts are inherent in any curriculum, they are not always explicitly stated. This lack of explication may well be due to a lack of certainty on the part of theoretical and applied linguists. There is certainly no widespread agreement within the profession about the nature of language and learning.

This confusion can be seen in relation to the concept of language proficiency. Not only is there confusion about concepts, linguists seem incapable of agreeing on terminology. From an inspection of the literature, one quickly comes to the conclusion that linguists are obsessed with conceptual universes in which creatures come in pairs. Thus, we have 'langue' and 'parole', 'competence' and 'performance', 'use' and 'usage', 'form' and 'meaning', 'context' and 'cotext', 'cohesion' and 'coherence'. It was Chomsky (1965) who gave prominence to the competence–performance distinction (although the theoretical distinction between the terms was not Chomsky's). For Chomsky, 'competence' refers to mastery of the principles governing language behaviour. 'Performance' refers to the manifestation of these internalised rules in actual language use. The terms have come to be used to refer to what a person knows about a language (competence) and what a person does (performance). More recently, the term 'communicative competence' has gained currency. This refers to knowledge of the rules of use and appropriacy and includes linguistic competence. While this might seem reasonably straightforward, there are a number of complicating factors. To begin with, there is nothing like universal agreement on what is meant by 'knowing'. Does 'knowing the rules of language' mean being able to recite them? If so, most native speakers must be classed as incompetent. According to Chomsky, however, native speakers are, by definition, competent.

Diller suggests:

> Linguists are sometimes hesitant to say that ordinary people 'know' the rules of their language, because linguists themselves have such a hard time trying to formulate these rules explicitly.
>
> (Diller 1978:26)

He points out that children can create phonological rules for nonsense words through a process of analogy, although they are unable to give a formulation for these rules. He goes on to ask:

> But if children are not able to formulate the rules of grammar which they use, in what sense can we say that they 'know' these rules? This is the question which has bothered linguists. The answer is that they know the rules in a functional way, in a way which relates the changes in abstract grammatical structure to changes in meaning. Knowledge does not always have to be formulated. Children can use tools before they learn the names for these tools.
>
> (*op cit.*:26–27)

For Diller then, knowledge need not be conscious but may manifest itself in the ability to use the language. However, this would seem to render the competence–performance distinction rather uncertain.

Krashen (1981, 1982) further confuses the issue by suggesting that knowledge of linguistic rules is the outward manifestation of one psychological construct (learning), while the manifestation of these rules in use is the manifestation of another construct (acquisition). Rea (1985) has since questioned the need for a 'competence' construct by suggesting that as we can observe only instances of performance, not competence, the competence–performance distinction is redundant. She brings this view into line with communicative language teaching by proposing yet another bifurcation; communicative performance and non-communicative performance.

It would seem, therefore, that we have reached a point where linguistic knowledge is to be defined in terms of what an individual is able to do with that knowledge. This is reinforced by a recent movement in ESL in the United States; competency-based ESL. As though there were not enough confusion over terminology, this movement is using 'competence' to refer to things learners can do with language; that is, it is used in roughly the same sense as 'performance' in the earlier competence–performance distinction. The concept of competency-based education (CBE) has been brought in to ESL from the field of adult education where it is used to specify the skills needed by adults to function in today's society in areas such as communication, computation, problem solving and interpersonal relationships.

In ESL, 'a competency is a task-oriented goal written in terms of behavioural objectives' (CAL 1983:9). The following characteristics of CBE as it relates to ESL have been articulated:

> Teaching ESL to competencies requires the instructional focus to be on functional competencies and life-coping skills. It is not what the students know about language but what they do with the language.
> Assessment is built in. Once the competency has been identified, it also serves as a means of evaluating student performance. Since it is performance based, assessment rests on whether the student can perform the competency or not. The only problem is to establish the level at which the student can perform the competency.
> Competencies are based on an assessment of student needs.
>
> (*op cit.*:11–13)

Within the literature, some writers use the term 'proficiency' as an alternative to 'competency' (see for example Higgs 1984). Richards, on the other hand, makes a clear distinction between 'competence' and 'proficiency', although he characterises the concept of proficiency in the same way as CBE characterises competency. This can be seen in the following quote:

> 1 When we speak of proficiency, we are not referring to knowledge of a language, that is, to abstract, mental and unobservable abilities. We are referring to performance, or, that is, to observable or measurable behaviour. Whereas competence refers to what we know about the rules of use and the rules of speaking of a language, proficiency refers to how well we can use such rules in communication.
> 2 Proficiency is always described in terms of real-world tasks, being defined with reference to specific situations settings purposes activities and so on.
> 3 In encapsulating the notion of skill, proficiency statements must always include a criterion.
> 4 It is assumed that proficiency in a given linguistic task involves the incorporating of a number of sub-skills or sub-tasks.

Richards goes on to say:

> A proficiency-oriented language curriculum is not one which sets
> out to teach learners linguistic or communicative competence, since
> these are merely abstractions or idealisations: rather, it is organised
> around the particular kinds of communicative tasks the learners
> need to master and the skills and behaviours needed to accomplish
> them. The goal of a proficiency-based curriculum is not to provide
> opportunities for the learners to 'acquire' the target language: it is
> to enable learners to develop the skills needed to use language for
> specific purposes.
>
> (Richards 1985a:5)

The foregoing discussion demonstrates the confusion surrounding a
number of key concepts relating to the nature of language. This confusion
is due partly to the inconsistent application of terms to concepts and
partly to confusion over the nature of the concepts themselves.

If the Richards line is followed, proficiency, simply put, refers to the
ability to perform real-world tasks with a pre-specified degree of skill.
For the moment we shall accept this definition, although it must be
pointed out that problems arise when the concept is probed a little more
rigorously. This will have to be done when we turn to the issue of the
assessment of language proficiency in Chapter 8. We shall see there that
the psychological reality of the construct 'proficiency' is itself problematic.

3.6   Towards a Generalised Language Curriculum Framework

In a recent study of curriculum processes Bartlett and Butler (1985)
propose a generalised curriculum framework which sets out five interde-
pendent but distinct categories. They call these categories the 'designed'
curriculum, the 'developed' curriculum, the 'enacted' curriculum, the
'received' curriculum and the 'assessed' curriculum. The designed curriculum contains a statement of the general philosophy and policy guiding
the curriculum. The developed curriculum consists of materials and the
articulation of processes which are meant to operationalise the designed
curriculum. The enacted curriculum consists of all the transactions between teachers and learners which are based on the materials and learning
processes derived from the developed curriculum. The received curriculum represents the outcomes of the curriculum process (what the
student actually learns).

It is often assumed that there exists a one-to-one relationship between
the planned, implemented and assessed curriculum. In other words, it
has been assumed that what is planned will be what gets taught, and

that what gets taught will be what is learned. This assumption grossly over-simplifies what is, in fact, an extremely complex set of processes.

The assumption has been criticised by Parlett and Hamilton in the following way:

> An instructional system, when it is adopted, undergoes modifications that are rarely trivial. The instructional system may remain as a shared idea, abstract model, slogan or shorthand, but it assumes a different form in every situation. Its constituent elements are emphasised or de-emphasised, expanded or truncated, as teachers, administrators, technicians and students interpret and reinterpret the instructional system for their particular setting. In practice, objectives are commonly reordered, redefined, abandoned or forgotten.
>
> (Parlett and Hamilton 1983:14)

By assuming that 'planning equals teaching equals learning', curriculum designers have focused on the planned, and, to a certain extent, the assessed curriculum, and have tended to ignore the implemented curriculum. It is only fairly recently that the balance has started to be redressed and that curriculum designers have become interested in classroom-based research. Such research is beginning to reveal to us the complexities of the curriculum in action.

3.7   The Teacher and the Curriculum

The Bartlett and Butler study introduced in the preceding section investigates the attempt to develop a learner-centred curriculum model at a national level. In order to capture the complexities of the processes set in train by the decision to embrace a learner-centred philosophy, Bartlett and Butler find it necessary to add a new element which they call the negotiated curriculum. The negotiated curriculum refers to those curriculum activities which involve negotiation and consultation between teachers and students. It includes such processes as needs analysis, jointly conducted goal and objective setting exercises by teachers and learners, negotiation of preferred methodology, materials and learning activities, and the sharing of evaluation and self-evaluation procedures.

The research questions which Bartlett and Butler set out to explore are as follows:

How are Adult Migrant Education Programs selected and arranged?
How are curriculum decisions made and implemented in the AMEP?
What support structures are available to personnel in the AMEP?
How is a needs-based approach to curriculum planning enacted in the
    classroom?

Data for the study were derived from a number of diverse sources which included documents, interview data, telephone consultancy data and data collected through the distribution of a questionnaire. Results of the data were ordered into an eight (States and Territories) by six (learning arrangements) by three (levels of decision making – national, state, local) matrix.

As a result of their study, Bartlett and Butler concluded that the learner-centred curriculum created a great deal of stress, that teachers were required to have a range of new skills if the ideals of the learner-centred curriculum were to become a reality, and that teachers required assistance and support in a number of areas. In particular, they concluded that assistance was required in the following areas:

> Needs assessment skills. The teachers require instruments and processes by which they can efficiently gather and prioritise student needs.
>
> Course guidelines. Teachers are asking for a broad framework within which they can negotiate the curriculum. They need to know what the students have done before and what will come after – in a form that does not stifle the negotiated curriculum.
>
> Course planning skills. The teachers are asking for planning skills that help them to negotiate a coherent, achievable set of objectives for a course, and then to plan a sequence of lessons to assist the students to attain the objectives.
>
> Bilingual help in negotiating the curriculum. The information exchange that is so crucial to the negotiated curriculum requires bilingual assistance in many classes.
>
> Continuity in the Programme. The needs-based model can easily give rise to a fragmented programme. Some teachers are caught in this bind and are asking for some form of programme management so that they feel their students are on a direct path to their goals.
>
> Educational counselling. In a needs-based model the size of the problem that confronts any individual teacher is directly related to the range and diversity of student needs. Teachers report that the negotiated curriculum becomes an impossible project if the student needs are very divergent. This is a key area where the teacher stress in negotiating the curriculum can be reduced – by forming a class group with a narrow range of needs. This requires the most efficacious use of educational counsellors, people who may themselves be curriculum developers, and who can direct students on a continuing basis into groups that match their needs.
>
> Conflict resolution. The opening up of the curriculum to negotiation will inevitably lead to some instances of conflict. The teachers reported in a survey that such conflict had arisen and many teachers had found suitable processes for resolving it.
>
> Teacher role specifications. The task of continually negotiating the curriculum with the students puts enormous strain on the teachers as is clearly evidenced in the survey.

(*op cit.*:112–113)

One of the issues raised by the Bartlett and Butler study, and, indeed, an issue underlying the adoption of a learner-centred approach to curriculum development with its implication of a greater professional burden on the classroom teacher, is the extent to which teachers see themselves as being responsible for the range of curriculum processes and activities that have been articulated in the preceding pages. In order to obtain supplementary evidence to that produced by Bartlett and Butler a survey was conducted of 35 teachers from a range of centre-based programmes in the Adult Migrant Education Program. The aim of the survey was to determine who, in the opinion of a representative group of teachers, should be principally responsible for carrying out initial and ongoing needs analysis, goal and objective setting, selecting and grading content, grouping learners, devising learning activities, instructing learners, monitoring and assessing learner progress and course evaluation.

The Study

Data were collected through the distribution of the survey form in Table 3.4.

TABLE 3.4 RESPONSIBILITY FOR CURRICULUM TASKS: SURVEY FORM

Indicate by giving a rating from 1 to 6 (1 = most important) who, in your opinion, should be primarily responsible for carrying out the following curriculum tasks. Give a rating from 1 to 6 for each curriculum task.

Key:

A   Counsellor
B   Bilingual resource person
C   Curriculum advisor
D   Teacher-in-charge of centre or program
E   Classroom teacher
F   Outside curriculum specialist

Curriculum processes	*A*	*B*	*C*	*D*	*E*	*F*
Initial needs analysis						
Goal and objective setting						
Selecting/Grading content						
Ongoing needs analysis						
Grouping learners						
Devising learning activities						
Instructing learners						
Monitoring/Assessing progress						
Course/evaluation						

Results

Rankings, from most to least important, for each of the curriculum tasks are set out in Table 3.5.

⟫→

TABLE 3.5 RESULTS OF SURVEY

Initial needs analysis

Classroom teacher
Bilingual resource person
Teacher-in-charge
Counsellor
Curriculum advisor
Outside curriculum specialist

Goal and objective setting

Classroom teacher
Curriculum advisor
Teacher-in-charge
Counsellor
Bilingual resource person
Outside curriculum specialist

Selecting and grading content

Classroom teacher
Curriculum advisor
Teacher-in-charge
Bilingual resource person
Counsellor
Outside curriculum specialist

Ongoing needs analysis

Classroom teacher
Teacher-in-charge
Bilingual resource person
Counsellor
Curriculum advisor
Outside curriculum specialist

Grouping learners

Teacher-in-charge
Classroom teacher
Counsellor
Curriculum advisor
Bilingual resource person
Outside curriculum specialist

Devising learning activities

Classroom teacher
Curriculum advisor
Outside curriculum specialist
Teacher-in-charge
Bilingual resource person
Counsellor

Instructing learners

Classroom teacher
Bilingual resource person
Outside curriculum specialist
Curriculum advisor
Teacher-in-charge
Counsellor

Monitoring/Assessing progress

Classroom teacher
Teacher-in-charge
Counsellor
Curriculum advisor
Bilingual resource person
Outside curriculum specialist

Course evaluation

Classroom teacher
Teacher-in-charge
Curriculum advisor
Outside curriculum specialist
Bilingual resource person
Counsellor

These data show quite clearly that the teachers surveyed saw themselves as having primary responsibility for all of the curriculum tasks except that of grouping learners. This reflects the fact that most teachers are simply not involved in the grouping process, which is unfortunate, as deriving appropriate groupings is one of the keys to successful learner-centred curriculum development.

The most important individuals after the classroom teacher were seen as the teacher-in-charge, and centre-based curriculum advisor. The scepticism of the classroom teacher towards outside curriculum specialists is evident from the generally low ranking given to such a person for most of the curriculum tasks.

It should be pointed out that the teachers who took part in this survey, unlike some others within the Adult Migrant Education Program, do not have access either to counsellors or bilingual resource persons, which may account for the comparatively low ratings given to them for some of the tasks. The fact that curriculum advisors did rather well, despite the fact that the teachers did not have access to such personnel either, suggests that the teachers perceive the need for 'on the ground' assistance in the curriculum area.

3.8 Summary

In this chapter, we have examined some of the theoretical and empirical foundations of a learner-centred approach to language curriculum development. These include theories of adult learning, communicative language teaching and the concept of language proficiency.

The chapter reports on three recent empirical investigations of teacher attitudes towards curriculum planning and communicative language teaching. For the group of teachers investigated, the concept of communicative language teaching is a salient one. The Bartlett and Butler study demonstrates some of the practical difficulties of developing a learner-centred model and indicates areas where teachers need assistance. The follow-up study indicates that teachers have accepted, in principle, the centrality of their place within an extended curriculum model.

4 Pre-Course Planning Procedures

4.1 Introduction

As we saw in the preceding chapter, the learner-centred curriculum has among other things a utilitarian rational: skills and knowledge are taught because the learner wishes to utilise them for some purpose beyond the learning environment itself, not simply because they happen to be part of a subject or academic discipline. This is not to say that those (principally foreign) language courses which do not have a utilitarian rationale are necessarily precluded from embracing principles of learner centredness, merely that applications to such programmes is often less apparent.

It has been suggested that content in the learner-centred curriculum should be justified in terms of relevance and motivational potential for the learner. A subject-centred approach to curriculum design often results in very similar content specifications for learners with widely differing needs. However, planning procedures within learner-centred systems need to be developed which have the potential for generating differentiated curricula for different learner types. In a sense, each course, generated as it is for a specific group of learners, is unique.

4.2 The Starting Point

The starting point for learner-centred curriculum development is generally the collection of various types of biographical data. These may include current proficiency level, age, educational background, previous language courses, nationality, marital status, the length of time spent in the target culture and previous, current and intended occupation. It may also include language, educational and life goals. Information can also be collected from learners on such subjective factors as the preferred length and intensity of a course, the preferred learning arrangement (whether the learner wants to engage in classroom or non-classroom based instruction), preferred methodology (which will include the types of materials and activities preferred by the learner), learning styles and general purpose in coming to class.

The first task in conducting a needs analysis is to decide on just what data need to be collected, when they should be collected, by whom, through what means and for what purpose or purposes.

Some information can be collected before a class starts. These data will probably include biographical information such as language proficiency, age, educational background and so on. They can be collected either by the teacher or by an educational counsellor through an interview which, with learners of low proficiency levels, will need to be conducted in the learner's first language, and will be used for initial grouping purposes. More subjective information, relating to methodology, learning-style preferences and materials, can generally be collected only once a given learning arrangement has been initiated.

4.3 Needs Analysis

During the 1970s, needs-analysis procedures made their appearance in language planning. While such procedures have a long tradition in other areas of adult learning, their use in language teaching became widespread with their adoption and espousal by The Council of Europe's modern language project. The principal proponents of the use of needs analysis were Richterich and Chancerel (see for example Richterich 1972, and Richterich and Chancerel 1978). In these Council of Europe documents needs analysis is used as the initial process for the specification of behavioural objectives. It is from these objectives that more detailed aspects of the syllabus such as functions, notions, topics, lexis and structural exponents are derived.

Richards suggests that needs analysis serves three main purposes: it provides a means of obtaining wider input into the content, design and implementation of a language programme; it can be used in developing goals, objectives and content; and it can provide data for reviewing and evaluating an existing programme (Richards 1984:5).

According to Richards, needs assessment has developed within a political climate which demands accountability and relevance in educational programmes. From this perspective, it can be seen as something which was foisted on the teaching profession, and which has little to do with educational values. There is some evidence that the technological rhetoric and systems thinking which accompanied needs-based programming has alienated some teachers, and in recent years it has been the pedagogical rather than the political value of undertaking needs analysis which has prompted its use in educational institutions.

Against this must be set Widdowson's (1987) suggestion that syllabuses which specify ends fulfil a training function and result in restricted competence. He contrasts such syllabuses with general-purposes syllabuses which, he claims, are process or means oriented, are educative in function and lead to general competence. It should be pointed out that these criticisms are basically logico-deductive rather than empirical. As yet, we simply do not know the extent to which ends-driven syllabuses are likely to facilitate or impede learning transfer.

Brindley addresses the issue of needs-based syllabus design from a rather different perspective, taking up a distinction made by Richterich (1972) between objective and subjective needs:

> The 'objective' needs are those which can be diagnosed by teachers on the basis of the analysis of personal data about learners along with information about their language proficiency and patterns of language use (using as a guide their own personal experience and knowledge, perhaps supplemented by Munby-type specifications of macro-skills), whereas the 'subjective' needs (which are often 'wants', 'desires', 'expectations', or other psychological manifestations of a lack) cannot be diagnosed as easily, or, in many cases, even stated by learners themselves.
>
> (Brindley 1984:31)

Objective needs analysis results in content specifications derived from an analysis of the target communicative situations in which learners are likely to find themselves. Being derived from an analysis of the target language situation, they can be carried out in the absence of the learner. Subjective needs, on the other hand, are derived from the learners themselves. While there is a tendency to equate objective needs with the specification of content, and subjective needs with the specification of methodology, the two need not be seen as synonymous. This is made clear in the following quote:

> While objective needs analysis and content are commonly linked, as are subjective needs and methodology, . . . it is, in fact, also possible to have a content/subjective needs dimension (learners deciding what they want to learn) and a methodology/objective needs dimension (teachers deciding how content might best be learned). The dimensions themselves are represented as a series of graduations rather then discrete categories.
>
> (Nunan 1985a:5)

The many and varied criticisms of needs-based planning, which include both ideological as well as practical objections, are reasonable enough as far as they go (some are more reasonable than others, some go further than others). However, recent critics have generally failed to appreciate the significant shift which has occurred over the years, and still tend to equate needs analysis with the sort of narrow-band ESP approach which typified the work of people such as Munby. For example Widdowson

(1983, 1987) suggests that needs-based courses will tend to result in formulaic 'phrase book' English, and will not develop in learners the ability to generate spontaneous communicative language.

However, as I pointed out in relation to the educative or training potential of means- and ends-driven syllabuses, whether or not courses developed to teach learners skills related to specific situations and events do result in language which is 'non-generative', or at least, less generative than courses in which input is selected on some other criteria, is a matter for empirical investigation. To my knowledge, such investigation has, as yet, to be carried out. In any case, the generative potential or otherwise of a given course would seem to rest more with the type of methodology employed than the criterion for content selection.

A second, more general, criticism is that needs analysis, or indeed any other form of pre-course planning and specification, is rather irrelevant because the planned curriculum will be transformed in its implementation. What really counts, therefore, in the development of second-language skills is the process of engaging learners in interesting and meaningful classroom experiences (see for example Krashen and Terrell 1983).

While one would not want to deny the importance of such experiences, it would seem that there is a better chance of these being interesting and meaningful if they are related in some way to the purposes to which learners wish to put their language skills.

In summary, needs analysis is a set of procedures for specifying the parameters of a course of study. Such parameters include the criteria and rationale for grouping learners, the selection and sequencing of course content, methodology, and course length, intensity and duration. In a learner-centred system, course designers will engage in extensive consultation with learners themselves in deriving parameters. Techniques for subjective needs analysis will therefore figure as prominently as techniques for objective needs analysis in such systems.

4.4   Participants in Pre-Course Planning Procedures

Ideally the key participants in pre-course planning should be the teachers who are to direct a course, and the learners who are to take part in it. Depending on the type of educational system and the resources available to it, other participants will include curriculum planners or advisors, counsellors and bilingual assistants. Each of these will be involved in collecting different types of information at different points in the life cycle of a course.

With learners who have little or no previous language-learning experience, information relating to learning preferences can be collected only once the course has begun and learners have had the opportunity of experiencing a variety of approaches. Such information is probably best collected informally by the teacher. With both experienced and inexperienced learners, it is desirable for the teacher to constantly monitor learners for changing needs and preferences. As learning should provide the opportunity for growth and development, all learners should be exposed to new methods, materials and approaches from time to time. However, this exposure should be carefully monitored, and learners should never be forced to engage in learning experiences to which they object. Such objections need not necessarily be articulated, and can often take the form of passive resistance. By building new learning experiences into courses, students will be sensitised to the learning process itself, and will have greater appreciation of what it is to be a learner. This, in turn, should facilitate the growth of learner autonomy. (An example of the important role which monitoring and negotiation can play in curriculum development is provided in the case study described in Chapter 10.)

Research is also currently being conducted to determine the extent to which exposure to new approaches, methods and materials is able to modify learners' preconceptions about appropriate learning activities. There are indications that developing more flexible and adaptive learning strategies is by no means as straightforward as it might at first seem, and that learners are more likely, initially at least, to adapt materials to their own learning schemata than to allow their schemata to be adapted by innovative materials and methods (Burton and Nunan 1986).

4.5   Grouping Learners

The sort of Munby-type needs analysis already described has an almost exclusive preoccupation with the 'objective' specification of course content. Other aspects of the curriculum development process such as learner groupings, methodology and evaluation are given very little attention. These aspects are either taken as given, or assumed to flow automatically from the specification of content.

One of the 'givens' in the Munby model is the learner. That is, it assumes that learners with particular needs will have been pre-identified or pre-specified by agents or processes outside the syllabus-design model itself. The key question for the curriculum designer thus becomes, 'Given a Spanish-speaking head waiter who is seeking work in an English-speaking restaurant', or, 'Given a Turkish engineer who wishes to undertake postgraduate study in an American university, what content should form the basis for an appropriate course?'

Such givens may or may not be adequate for narrowly-focused ESP-type courses. However, most second language teaching institutions have relatively heterogeneous client groups. Any student intake may include learners who range from tertiary graduates to learners who are illiterate, even in their own language. In such institutions, the major initial purpose for collecting learner data is to group learners in appropriate ways. At present, it seems that proficiency level on intake is the most commonly used grouping criterion. It is assumed by teachers (and learners) that effective language learning can only take place in classes that are relatively homogeneous in terms of student proficiency level. (Recent research into second-language acquisition in the classroom is beginning to question this conventional wisdom; see for example Long and Porter 1985.) However, the fact remains that teachers consistently nominate mixed proficiency groups as the most difficult to plan for adequately (Watts 1985).

In order to derive more sensitive learner groupings, it is important to see beyond the '20 student syndrome'. This syndrome equates 'classes' with 20 to 30 students, all meeting as a group for a predetermined number of hours a week. While such thinking is convenient from an administrative perspective, it severely limits the potential of the teaching institution. This is particularly true in smaller language schools or centres which may only have the equivalent of six or seven full-time classes. While the larger the centre the greater the potential for more sensitive learner groupings, it is possible to innovate in smaller centres (Brink *et al.* 1985).

In a language centre in which class groupings are based on the traditional '20 plus' lines according to proficiency level, a given student is likely to spend most of his week in a single class with 20 or so other learners. In a more flexible learning arrangement, however, he is likely to be placed in a range of classes during the day or week and will thus come into contact with a greater range of teachers and fellow learners. At the beginning of each day, for instance, the student might be in a 'home' group based on proficiency level. At other times however, he might be in groups selected on the basis of intended occupation, learning style preference, or macro-skill focus. In one small programme which changed recently from a traditional to a learner-centred curriculum, it was found that, instead of having five class groups for its 120 students, there were 23 'classes' in the weekly timetable. Needless to say, this greatly complicated the business of timetabling, and had implications for staffing, room availability and so on. The experiment did demonstrate, however, that more flexible groupings are possible and that administrative obstacles can be overcome.

It should be obvious that a learner-centred curriculum can succeed only with the support of programme administrators, and with decisions on grouping learners being made at centre or school level, rather than at individual teacher level. A teacher working alone, and trying to derive more sensitive within-class grouping, will experience severe difficulties and will be able to succeed only to a limited extent. The more teachers and students who are involved in developing the curriculum, the more successful it is likely to be. This is not to say that within-class groupings are not important, merely that curriculum decision making will be much more effective if it is a joint venture undertaken by teachers and administrators at centre level.

While initial data collection is used for grouping learners, both initial and ongoing data collection are used for content selection and the selection of learning materials and experiences. In specifying and grading content, consideration will need to be given to such things as language skills, structures, functions, notions, topics, themes, situations and interlocutors. If these are selected according to the needs of the learner, there is likely to be some variation from learner group to learner group. Content selection and grading will be considered in detail in the next chapter.

Ongoing data collection, which will most often take the form of informal monitoring and teacher observation, can be used to select materials and learning experiences which accord with the needs and interests of the learners. These are considered in greater detail in Chapter 6.

In this section we have looked at the uses to which data gathered through needs analysis are put. The major purposes are in grouping learners at centre level, in organising sub-groups within classes, in deriving language content and in selecting appropriate materials and learning activities.

4.6   Resources for Planning

Techniques for data collection and course planning can be ranged on a continuum from formal to informal. Formal techniques include standardised interviews and proficiency assessments, while informal techniques include such things as classroom observation and self-rating scales for use by learners in evaluating learning activities. Some of these techniques are presented here, while others are presented in Chapter 8.

It is highly desirable in educational systems which have significant numbers of low-proficiency learners, that a range of bilingual and first-language resources be available. In the study described in Chapter 10, many of the problems attributed to the curriculum were, in fact, due to the lack of information available to learners about the learning experiences they were undergoing.

In one recent study into the use of the learner's first language in second-language learning, O'Grady and Kang found that:

> The provision of a learner-centred system which assists clients to define their educational goals and offers courses in response to their expressed needs . . . can be effected only through clear channels of communication between learner and course provider. . . . The

achievement of a learner-centred system is dependent on a mechanism whereby L1 access is available as a matter of course to define clients' needs and to facilitate their ongoing control of their learning.

(O'Grady and Kang 1985:23)

Forms such as the one in Table 4.1 are useful at centre level for documenting and keeping track of data-collection procedures:

TABLE 4.1

Data	When collected?	By whom?	How?	For what purpose?
Proficiency level				
Age				
Educational background				
Previous courses				
Nationality				
Marital status				
Time in country				
Occupation				
First language				
Other languages				
Preferred course length				
Preferred learning arrangement				
Preferred methodology				
Learning style				
Language goals				
Life goals				

It will be noted that the information solicited falls naturally into two different categories. The first is essential biographical information, while the second is more personal, relating to the learners' preferences and perception of need. The first would normally be collected during pre-course interviews, while the second would generally be collected informally by the teacher during the first weeks of the course.

There are many different interview formats available for identifying learner needs. Some of these are more comprehensive than others. In order to provide some idea of the sorts of detailed information which can be collected for planning purposes see the Appendix.

At the initial data-collection stage, most classroom teachers would probably wish to collect only a fraction of the data listed in the Appendix. As a minimum, however, it would probably be desirable to collect information on target communication tasks and situations and preferences regarding learning activities, macro-skill focus and within-class groupings.

One teacher who habitually solicits preferences from her students provided the data set out in Table 4.2. She obtained the data from her students at the beginning of a class by getting them to complete a questionnaire according to a four-point scale. The results enabled her, in the initial stages of the course, to plan activities which were in line with the learners' expressed needs.

TABLE 4.2 SUBJECTIVE LEARNING PREFERENCES OBTAINED FROM ONGOING STUDENTS AT THE BEGINNING OF A LEARNING ACTIVITY. (ACTIVITIES ARE RANKED IN ORDER OF DESCENDING IMPORTANCE.)

A. *For what communicative situations and tasks do you wish to learn English?*

1   Talking in formal situations (e.g. to the doctor)
2   Understanding the radio and television
3   Filling in forms
4   Understanding native speakers
5   Reading newspapers
6   Understanding the Australian way of life
7   Writing letters
8   Talking to friends and neighbours

B. *What learning activities do you prefer?*

1   Learning grammar rules
2   Pronunciation
3   Learning new words
4   Studying a textbook or coursebook

C. *Which skills are most important for you?*

1   Speaking
2   Listening
3   Writing
4   Reading

D. *What sort of groupings do you prefer?*

1   Practising with the whole class
2   Practising in small groups
3   Practising in pairs
4   Studying alone

The data were important for the teacher for a number of reasons. For example, the low rating given by learners to the use of pair work was something the teacher had to address as it had been her intention to base most communicative classroom practice on such pair work.

4.7   Investigating Needs-Analysis Procedures

In 1984, a major investigation of the needs-analysis and objective-setting practices within one state Adult Migrant Education Service was carried out by Brindley and Bagshaw. In this section we shall look at some aspects of the study which is reported in detail in Brindley (1984).

Background

The study was established with the following brief:
– to identify the general issues and principles of needs analysis and objective setting consistent with current understanding of adult language learning and with AMEP methodology in particular
– to document existing practices in the areas of needs analysis and objective setting
– to propose a system for categorising the long-term language goals of learners
– to investigate mechanisms for translating these long-term goals into specific short-term objectives that are attainable within the scope of one course or learning arrangement
– to identify processes by which these objectives could be identified and articulated by the learner and agreed to by learner and teacher
– to identify the implications for teacher training and materials development in implementing such a system or systems
– to identify areas of further research.

Methodology

Methodology for the study included a literature study; quantitative data collection from various stake-holders in the educational enterprise including learners, teachers, administrators and bilingual information officers; and finally, comparison of current practices and attitudes with the general principles extracted from the literature.

Learner variables which were hypothesised to 'affect the awareness of learners and the extent to which they are able to articulate their language-learning needs' included the following:
– first language
– sex

- ethnicity
- age
- education
- occupational background
- length of residence in the target culture
- intended residence in the target culture
- status of the individual within the family
- urban/rural background.

Results

There is no space here to provide a comprehensive summary of either the study or the results obtained. For our purposes, the following results are pertinent.

In general, and contrary to a great deal of popular opinion, learners were able to articulate long-term goals, and to provide instrumental reasons for attending language classes. Many of them also had clear (and fairly fixed) ideas about what it was to learn a language, and what were legitimate activities in the language class. The fact that many of these appear to be at odds with current communicative practices is taken up in Chapter 6.

Finally, comprehensive and systematic data-collection processes for the purposes of deriving content and methodology did not seem to characterise the educational system under investigation. In this regard, the study concluded that:

> Although it appears that most teachers are attempting to cater for learners' needs in some way, the fact that they hold these differing views of needs means that there is little uniformity in the way in which information about learners is collected and used in programming. Similarly, the extent to which learners are involved in formulating their own objectives varies widely, ranging from courses planned in consultation to those planned entirely by the teacher with no input from learners.
>
> (Brindley 1984:iv)

4.8   Conclusion

In this chapter, we have looked at some initial pre-course planning procedures. The central processes here are initial data collection and the deriving of learner groupings. Deriving appropriate learner groups is a critically important task. In Chapter 10, it will be seen that one of the greatest problems for the teacher as curriculum developer is having to construct a coherent programme for inappropriately grouped learners.

It has been claimed that one important outcome of involving learners in ongoing curriculum development is that not only does it increase the likelihood that the course will be perceived as relevant, but learners will be sensitised to their own preferences, strengths and weaknesses. They will become more aware of what it is to be a learner, will develop skills in 'learning how to learn' and will be in a better position to negotiate the curriculum in the future. The empirical study reported in the body of the chapter indicates that learners are, in fact, capable of becoming involved in the planning of their own learning experiences.

The adoption of a more subjective orientation will necessitate a shift away from the sorts of 'technocratic' procedures inherent in the Munby needs-analysis model to less formal procedures for both sensitising learners and obtaining input from them for developing the curriculum. These procedures should be conducted continually throughout a given learning arrangement, rather than occurring only in the initial stages.

In the next chapter, we shall look at some of the ways in which initial planning and data collection can be utilised in specifying content.

5 *Planning Content*

5.1 Introduction

There are many possible starting points for deriving course content. Rowntree suggests that these can be divided into informal (or intuitive) approaches and systematic (or analytical) approaches. He goes on to say:

> Broadly speaking, the intuitive approaches are those that give us most help in thinking up possible content in the first place. The analytical techniques, on the other hand, tend to be most useful once we have generated a few ideas and are ready to see how they hang together and can be extended. In reality, of course, we are thinking both intuitively and analytically at all stages of course planning. Sometimes one predominates, however, and sometimes the other.
>
> (Rowntree 1981:35)

Examples provided by Rowntree of intuitive approaches to content specification include:

- sitting and reviewing one's own knowledge of the proposed subject
- asking other teachers and subject-matter experts
- analysing similar courses elsewhere
- reviewing textbooks aimed at students working at about the same level as ours will be
- reading more advanced books and scholarly articles on the subject
- reviewing films, radio and television tapes, newspaper and popular journal articles, etc. relating to the proposed subject
- asking prospective students what they would like to see the course include
- discussing with students their existing conceptions of, and attitudes to, the key concepts of the subject matter
- choosing books (or other source material) around which the course will be organised
- thinking of essential activities that students need to engage in as part of the course
- considering how student attainment on the course might most sensibly be assessed

– studying an examination syllabus, the question papers, and examiners' reports from previous years, and so on.

(*op cit.*:35–36)

5.2   Content Selection – An Empirical Investigation

In this section, we shall look briefly at a study set up to determine how teachers operating in a learner-centred system determine input for their courses.

Background

Evidence from other subject areas (such as those cited by Rowntree) suggests that teachers use a variety of sources for deriving course content. Anecdotal evidence suggests that for most language teachers whose learners do not vary significantly from one course to the next, content selection is largely a matter of refining input from course to course rather than starting from scratch every time. The input selection phase of curriculum planning is thus an evolutionary one.

Ideally, in a learner-centred system, content should be derived through a process of consultation and negotiation with the learners, the principal consideration being the communicative needs of the learners. (We looked at procedures for determining such needs in Chapter 4.)

The Study

In an investigation into how teachers actually do select content, a group of adult ESL teachers (n = 28) were asked to nominate the procedures they followed in identifying course content. The teachers, who were all highly experienced, were asked to complete a questionnaire during the course of an in-service programme on course design.

Procedure

In order to prompt the teachers to review the means whereby they selected input, they were asked to imagine that they had just been assigned a group of learners whose data profiles were different from any learners they had ever worked with before. The questionnaire is set out in Table 5.1:

⟫⟶

TABLE 5.1 SURVEY QUESTIONNAIRE

---

*Which of the following learner groups have you **never** worked with before? (Circle the appropriate number.)*

A.   Zero proficiency learners who are illiterate in their own language.
B.   Advanced students who want a pre-tertiary course.
C.   Learners who are studying in the English-in-the-Workplace program.
D.   Fast track On-Arrival students.
E.   Mixed level students in the Community Program.

Imagine you have been assigned one of the groups you have circled. How would you go about determining course content? Select three of the following options.

1   Devising learning activities and tasks
2   Drawing on knowledge of language and language learning
3   Consulting other teachers with relevant experience
4   Selecting a coursebook
5   Determining post-course communication needs
6   Analysing other relevant language courses
7   Selecting appropriate materials
8   Consulting and negotiating with learners on course content

---

Results

Rankings for the questionnaire items are set out in Table 5.2:

TABLE 5.2 RESULTS OF QUESTIONNAIRE ON CONTENT SELECTION

Item	Rank
1 Devising learning activities and tasks	5
2 Drawing on knowledge of language and language learning	3
3 Consulting other teachers	2
4 Selecting a coursebook	7
5 Determining post-course communication needs	1
6 Analysing other relevant language courses	8
7 Selecting appropriate materials	6
8 Consulting and negotiating with learners	3

Discussion

From the data, it would seem that teachers who are accustomed to working within a learner-centred system do indeed take as their starting point the learners and their communicative needs. Whether, in fact, they actually do consult learners and carry out communicative needs analyses is another question. The fact that they were prepared to place Items 5 and 8 relatively high on their list of priorities indicates that the concept of a learner-centred approach to content selection was taken seriously by the teachers who took part in the study. In actual fact, these data conflict to a certain extent with data yielded in the interviews carried out as part of the study reported in Chapter 10. There, teachers who had actually been confronted with unfamiliar students stated that they either consulted more experienced colleagues or looked to a coursebook for ideas on content. (See also the case study in Chapter 10.)

In a follow-up discussion, the teachers, when questioned on the degree to which they would actually do what they said, affirmed that they would. However, they also registered the familiar objection to forced-choice questionnaires, stating that they might, in fact, use all eight means of determining content. During the course of the study reported in Chapter 10, it became apparent that teachers objected to providing data that was easily quantifiable on the grounds that it forced them to distort the reality of their day-to-day curriculum practices. The implications of this attitude for curriculum research and evaluation is discussed in the final chapter.

5.3   Analytical Approaches to Content Specification

According to Rowntree, analytical approaches to content selection include such things as task, concept and competency analysis. These approaches would be used by someone following the Munby approach to course design. Also included as an analytical approach is the use of objectives. While acknowledging the difficulty many teachers have with the 'objectives first' approach, Rowntree says:

> I still believe they [objectives] are extremely valuable in course development. Asking oneself what students should be able to do by the end of the course that they could not do (or not do so well) at the beginning can be highly illuminating. Many teachers (and I am one) would claim their teaching has been far better since they were introduced to objectives.
>
> (*op cit*.:35)

However, he acknowledges that one need not necessarily start with the specification of objectives and that this may, in fact, be one of the last tasks undertaken in course planning.

Traditional subject-centred approaches to language course design have selected input on the basis of some form of linguistic content analysis. Such analyses result in lists of structural and lexical items which are graded according to linguistic notions of complexity and difficulty, and counts of lexical frequency.

The development of functional–notional syllabuses represented more a broadening of focus than a paradigm shift. While such syllabuses pay more attention to the purposes to which language is put, they are still basically subject- rather than learner-centred, with content specification resulting from the introspection of linguists rather than on empirical investigation of the uses to which users actually do put language in different contexts. This broadened focus has, however, made content selection and grading much more complex than hitherto. One comprehensive document, *Threshold Level English* (van Ek and Alexander 1980), specifies the following components:

- the situations in which the foreign language will be used, including the topics which will be dealt with
- the language activities in which the learner will engage
- the language functions which the learner will perform
- topics, and what the learner will be able to do with these
- the general notions which the learner will be able to handle
- the specific (topic related) notions which the learners will be able to handle
- the language forms the learner will be able to use
- the degree of skill the learner will be required to display.

Many teachers have found that a useful means of generating integrated and relevant content is by using as a starting point the data derived from learners at the initial planning stage. For this procedure to work, however, it is necessary to have a reasonably homogeneous group of learners to start with.

Much of the confusion and uncertainty surrounding the specification of content stems from the proliferation of input parameters. We have just seen that the authors of *Threshold Level English* identify at least eight such parameters. Given this proliferation, the key problem is one of knowing where to start. Many recent courses and syllabus outlines start with a listing of functions, and fit the other components around this. The problem with such an approach is that it generally results in a syllabus which is little more than a listing of discrete items which are graded either according to the syllabus designer's intuitive notions of simplicity and complexity, or according to utilitarian notions of what is likely to be of most use to the learner. Such syllabus listings are open to many of the criticisms which have been levelled against structural syllabuses.

By starting with learner goals, and using these to derive content, much of the disorganisation entailed in the functional approaches can be obviated. In such a procedure, the specification of functions, structures, lexis and so on are derived as a result of the prior specification of the communicative goals which the learner will need to master in the given domains of language use. They are therefore an end product, rather than a starting point in the design process.

One of the most contentious issues in course planning concerns the use of objectives. There are many different ways in which the objectives of a course of study can be stated. They can be set out in terms of what the teacher plans to do in class, in terms of the general goals and philosophy of the teaching institution, in terms of course content, or in terms of what the learner is expected to be able to do at the end of a course of study. In a survey of current objective-setting practice, Brindley discovered that, 'The overwhelming majority of examples given were expressed as teacher objectives' (Brindley 1984:56). Examples of the types of objectives articulated by teachers are as follows:

> Instructional Goals: to develop learners' confidence in speaking and listening
> Course Descriptions/Descriptions of Language Content: to provide input in real, relevant and realistic Australian English
> Learning Materials: to present an episode of 'The Man Who Escaped'.
>
> (*op cit.*:56–57)

Most of the controversy in general education has concerned the use of behavioural or, as they are now more commonly known, performance objectives. These have been defined in a number of different ways. Valette and Disick (1972) suggest that they should stress output rather than input and that such output should be specified in terms of performance. It has been suggested that precise statements of what the learner is to be able to do at the end of a course is an essential step in the curriculum-design process which greatly facilitates a number of other steps. It forces the designer to be realistic about what a given learner or group of learners can hope to achieve. It also helps guide the selection of appropriate materials and learning activities, and is an essential prerequisite to evaluation.

Gronlund suggests that performance objectives will help a teacher strike the correct balance in developing a course. He states that:

> All too frequently, little attention is paid to determining precisely and specifically what type of pupil performance is desired at the end of an instructional sequence. As a result, one of two extreme

situations typically exists. In the one case, intended outcomes are
limited to the learning of material covered in a textbook and teaching
and evaluation procedures are primarily concerned with the
retention of textbook content. At the other extreme, overly
ambitious goals are set for a course – goals so general and so
idealistic that they are impossible either to achieve or evaluate. The
reason that these two situations are so common is probably because
the task of clearly defining instructional objectives appears
gargantuan and therefore overwhelming. It need not be, despite
some admitted complexities. Furthermore, rewards in terms of more
effective teaching, learning and evaluation are great.

(Gronlund 1981:29)

In the field of general education, the use of performance objectives has
come under heavy criticism (see for example Macdonald-Ross 1975 and
Stenhouse 1975). These criticisms, however, need to be seen in the socio-
political and educational context within which they were made. Thus
the criticisms of Stenhouse are made within an educational system where
structure and coherence are provided by the traditional subjects in the
school curriculum. His criticisms are also aimed at the use of objectives
in subjects which have as their aim the development of knowledge and
aesthetic sensibilities and, in fact, he suggests that for language learning
the use of objectives may well be a valid procedure.

Studies in mainstream education indicate that most teachers simply
do not plan their courses by starting with the generation of objectives
(Shavelson and Stern 1981). However, those teachers who have
homogeneous enough groups to utilise objectives find they have all the
advantages suggested by Gronlund. One teacher, working in an English
in the workplace programme, who took part in the study reported in
detail in Chapter 10, stated that:

We can see the value of setting objectives that are attainable, and
we have built time into the programme to do this.

The operative word here, of course, is 'time'. It takes time to plan
coherent courses, and it is probably lack of time, rather than ideological
objections, which prevents teachers developing clear objectives.

A procedure which some teachers have found useful is to start by
deriving tasks and skills from learner goals. These skills provide an
integrative framework, and appropriate topics, contexts and materials,
which are derived from an analysis of learner data, can be incorporated
into the framework. A sample number of performance objectives can
then be derived from the resulting planning grid. These are extremely
useful when it comes to assessing learner progress. (An example of how
this procedure might work is provided in the next section.)

In a learner-centred curriculum, specifying course objectives, can, if these are conveyed to the learners, play an important part in the process of sensitising learners to what it is to be a language learner. By making explicit course objectives, the following benefits can accrue:

Learners come to have a more realistic idea of what can be achieved in a given course.
Learning comes to be seen as the gradual accretion of achievable goals.
Students develop greater sensitivity to their role as language learners and their rather vague notions of what it is to be a learner become much sharper.
Self-evaluation becomes more feasible.
Classroom activities can be seen to relate to learners' real-life needs.
The development of skills can be seen as a gradual rather than an all-or-nothing process.

It is generally considered that objectives need to include a task statement, a conditions statement and a standards statement (see for example Valette and Disick 1972; Mager, 1975; Gronlund 1981). The task statement specifies what the learner is required to do, the conditions statement specifies the conditions under which the task will be performed and the standards statement specifies the standard to be achieved.

The focus of the task can vary, as can be seen in the following examples:

Grammatical focus: Learners will use Wh-questions in controlled drills.
Functional focus: Learners will express agreement and disagreement.
Macro-skill focus: Learners will identify the main point in a spoken text.
Learning skills focus: Learners will monitor and rate their performance on spoken tasks.
Cognitive focus: Learners will extract relevant information from a spoken text and label the accompanying diagram.
Cultural focus: Learners will compare behaviour in an interview situation with that in their native country.
Topical focus: Learners will obtain relevant information about public transport.

Tasks can also be classified according to whether they refer to performance in the real world (the learner will complain about an unsatisfactory purchase) or the classroom (the learner will listen to an aural text and note down key words). Another distinction which is sometimes made is between product-oriented tasks, which specify what learners will be able to do as a result of instruction, and process-oriented tasks, which specify the activities to be undertaken during instruction.

In the next section, we shall examine one way in which skills can be derived from learner data, and how these, in turn, can be used to produce specific performance objectives for learner assessment. The remainder of the chapter will be devoted to the problem of grading content.

5.4   Deriving Content from Learner Data

In this section, we shall look at a procedure for deriving content from learner data. There are two different ways in which the process to be described can be utilised. One of these is to treat each intake of learners as unique, and to construct a programme anew, from the ground up, as it were, for each group. A more realistic approach is for a language centre to identify recurring learner types and to prepare general course outlines which can be utilised with successive intakes of students. For any centre following this second procedure, it would be necessary to add and delete course outlines as the client profile changed.

The first step in the process is to examine learner data and extract information relating to the purposes for which learners are attending the course and which can be translated into communicative goals. This information will more often than not be expressed in fairly general, functional terms. Examples of the sorts of goals which are commonly expressed are as follows:

I would like to be able to:
- talk to my neighbours
- find out about Australian culture
- read newspapers
- understand TV and radio
- fill out forms
- read signs and notices
- talk to my daughter's teacher
- read stories in English to my grandchildren
- undertake tertiary study in English
- understand people in the workplace.

If the curriculum is being developed at a centre level, this information can be used to develop modules or ᵗeaching strands. If it is being used at an individual classroom level, the teacher will need to decide on which goals take priority. Ideally, the learners themselves should be involved in prioritisation through a process of consultation and negotiation.

The second step in the process is to specify the communicative tasks and enabling skills which learners will need to be able to perform in order to achieve their language goals. These can often be generalised across goals, courses or modules. For example, three of the goals identified above relate to the real-world task of having a conversation (talk to my neighbours, talk to my daughter's teacher, understand people in the workplace). For a given proficiency level, each of these would conceivably have similar subordinate task and enabling skill specifications. At a post-beginner level these could include the following:

— identify topic of conversation
— signal lack of comprehension
— exchange greetings/leave-taking
— comprehend requests for personal information
— provide personal details
— indicate likes and dislikes
— request factual information
— describe objects/entities
— offer and ask for help
— check that one had comprehended correctly
— check that one had been correctly comprehended.

While some of these tasks are similar to the headings commonly found in functional syllabuses, they differ from such syllabuses in that they are drawn together under a particular goal statement. They therefore provide a more coherent framework than is provided by general functional syllabuses.

The next step is to provide contextualisation for the tasks by deciding on such things as topics, settings, interlocutors and so on. These data, which can be derived from needs analyses, serve to differentiate goals for different learner groups.

The specifications derived at this stage can be combined with the list of tasks and skills to produce planning grids. The sample grid in Table 5.3 utilises the elements already specified for the development of conversational skills (overleaf).

The next step in the content specification process is to decide on linguistic elements (i.e. the notions, structures, lexis and so on) which will need to be taught in order for learners to be able to operationalise the pre-specified skills. There is, in fact, some debate as to whether this step is necessary. It could be argued that, if we specify and teach to communicative tasks, the linguistic exponents will look after themselves. This, along with so many of the issues raised in this work, is a matter which demands empirical investigation.

There are, in fact, two issues here. One is a syllabus-design issue, the other is basically methodological. The syllabus-design issue is whether or not a course should be grammatically structured. The methodological issue is whether or not grammatical structures should be consciously taught. Any of the four following conditions could obtain:

1 The course is grammatically sequenced and the grammatical points are explicitly taught.

TABLE 5.3

| | Contexts | | | | | |
	1	2	3	4	5	6
Identify topic of conversation						
Signal lack of comprehension						
Exchange greeting/leave-taking						
Comprehend requests for personal information						
Provide personal details						
Indicate likes and dislikes						
Request factual information						
Describe objects and entities						
Offer and ask for help						
Check comprehension						

KEY:
1 Classroom   3 Neighbourhood   5 Child's school
2 Interview   4 Supermarket   6 Post office

2 The course is grammatically sequenced but the grammatical points are not explicitly taught.
3 The course is not grammatically sequenced, but grammatical points are explicitly taught as they arise.
4 The course is not grammatically sequenced, and no explicit teaching of grammar occurs.

The question of whether or not courses should be structurally graded is a complex one, and one which will certainly not be solved here. The name most commonly associated with the non-graded or 'natural' approach is Krashen (1981, 1982), who based his arguments on the assertions that grading is unnecessary because classroom input which is interesting, meaningful and relevant will automatically be at an appropriate order of difficulty, and that a graded syllabus will lead to a focus on meaning not form (he is arguing, in effect, that Situation 2, where we have a graded course, but no focus on form will not obtain). These arguments are comprehensively critiqued in Pienemann (1985). To repeat, arguments as to whether structurally-graded courses and explicit grammar teaching lead to more effective learning will only be settled in the long term by empirical investigations rather than the sorts of theoretical arguments advanced by some applied linguists. Common sense would suggest that explicit instruction will be beneficial for some learners but not others.

The final task in the procedure described here is to produce a sample number of specific objectives which are related, via tasks/skills, to learner goals. By producing such objectives, one will have a set of ready-made criteria for judging the effectiveness of the learning process. This step therefore provides a convenient bridge into the assessment and evaluation phase of the curriculum-development process.

It was pointed out earlier in the chapter that specific objectives contain three elements: tasks, conditions and standards. The task statement indicates what it is that the learner is to do; the conditions define the circumstances under which the task will be carried out; and the standards specify the degree of skill to be exhibited.

Here are two examples of specific objectives derived from the preceding specifications.

Enabling Skill: Exchange greetings/leave-taking
Specific objective: In a classroom role play, students will exchange greetings with the teacher. Utterances will be comprehensible to someone used to dealing with a second language speaker.
Task: exchange greetings with the teacher
Conditions: in a classroom role play
Standards: utterances to be comprehensible to someone used to dealing with a second-language speaker

≫→

Communicative Task: Request factual information
Specific objective: In an authentic interaction, students will request
  prices of shopping items. Questions will be comprehensible to a
  sympathetic native speaker.
Task: request prices of shopping items
Conditions: in an authentic interaction
Standards: utterances to be comprehensible to a sympathetic native
  speaker.

In fact, it may not always be necessary to specify conditions and standards
for every single performance objective. An alternative is to specify sets
of conditions and standards for a given module, teaching strand or class
which will apply to all objectives. (For further details on this see Nunan
1985b.)

5.5   Grading Content

Once the content for a course or module has been specified, it needs to
be sequenced. This creates a whole new set of problems. These problems,
and possible solutions to them, are examined in this section.

One alternative to the problem of grading is to have no sequence at
all, to treat each lesson as a self-contained unit or module. This, in fact,
is an alternative which is forced upon teachers who operate in institutions
with an open entry/exit policy (that is, a policy which allows students
to enter or leave a given course at any time).

Most curriculum designers, however, operate on the assumption that
a course will consist of a sequence of lessons which need to be structured
and graded in some way, and that their client group of learners will be
relatively stable for the duration of the course.

In his general consideration of course structuring, Rowntree has this
to say:

> Our interest in sequence arises because the student cannot learn
> everything at once. If he is to learn A and B, he must either learn
> A and then B, or B first and then A. Unless he can learn a little bit
> of A and then B (but how much and in what order?) . . . But these
> may not be equally viable alternatives. For any given student, one
> of these sequences may be better – more 'learnable' than others.
> . . . So, in enquiring about sequence, we are really asking whether
> one way of ordering the content of a course will be more helpful,
> educationally, than any other possible order.
>
> (Rowntree 1981:106)

The issue of sequencing was less complicated (but by no means unprob-
lematic) when course content was largely derived from linguistic struc-

tures. Decisions about whether to teach A before B were made according to linguistic notions of simplicity and complexity. If item A were considered to be simpler linguistically than structure B, then it was taught first. (Recent investigations by second-language acquisition researchers have demonstrated that, in fact, these notions were not particularly accurate, and that there are discrepancies between what is difficult in terms of a given grammatical model, and what learners actually find difficult in terms of their psycholinguistic processing capacity. Thus the 'third person -s' morpheme is grammatically simple but psycholinguistically complex.)

With the adoption of a communicative orientation, the tasks of structuring and grading become much more complex. It will be recalled that this view conceives of language learning as a process of learning to do things with language. It is therefore behavioural and task-based. Grading tasks, from this perspective, means specifying degrees of skill as well as describing performance. Levels of skill and task complexity consist of complex clusters of factors. These will include the following:

- the degree to which the language event is embedded in a context which facilitates comprehension
- the degree to which the language event makes cognitive demands on the learner. (Presumably, identifying a named item by pointing to it is cognitively less demanding than describing it.)
- the degree to which the background knowledge of the language user can be utilised to assist in comprehension
- the amount of assistance provided to the language learner. (It is reasonable to assume that conveying a message to a native speaker who is sympathetic towards, and used to dealing with, second-language learners is easier than attempting to convey the same message to an unsympathetic interlocutor.)
- the processing difficulty of the language. (This is the only factor on which we have a reasonable amount of empirical evidence.)
- the degree of stress experienced by the learner in taking part in a language event. (Presumably, conveying a message to a friend is less stressful than making a speech in front of 500 people.)

The role of factors such as those listed above in determining task difficulty is discussed in Clark (1985b).

Brindley (in Nunan 1987a) has suggested that learner, task and text factors will interact to determine task difficulty. He suggests that the factors in Table 5.4 will need to be considered in grading objectives:

》》→

TABLE 5.4

1 Learner factors	Questions to consider	Comments/Examples
Confidence	How confident does the learner have to be to carry out the task? Does the learner have the necessary level of confidence?	Some tasks may require high levels of confidence, e.g. initiating interaction with a member of the public as part of a community interaction activity.
Motivation	How motivating is the task?	Some learners may be unmotivated to undertake certain kinds of tasks which do not appear to be personally relevant or interesting, e.g. drills or games.
Prior learning experience	Does the task assume familiarity with certain learning skills? Does the learner's prior learning experience provide the necessary learning skills/strategies to carry out the task?	Some tasks may assume familiarity with particular ways of learning, e.g. skills in inducing general rules from examples.
Learning pace	How much learning material has the learner shown s/he is capable of handling? Is the task broken down into manageable parts?	Learning pace will obviously vary from individual to individual and is not related to proficiency level.

1 Learner factors	Questions to consider	Comments/Examples
Observed ability in language skills	What is the learner's assessed level in the skill(s) concerned? Does this assessment conform to his/her observed behaviour in class? In the light of the teacher's assessment, what overall level of performance can reasonably be expected?	Proficiency descriptions (ASLPR, AMES, ACTFL, etc.) give a general indication of the characteristics of language behaviour at different levels of ability. The descriptions can assist in deciding the sort of language behaviour that can be expected at a given level.
Cultural knowledge/ awareness	Does the task assume cultural knowledge? If so, can the learner be expected to have it? Does the task assume knowledge of a particular subject?	Some tasks assume a good deal of cultural knowledge (e.g. interpreting newspaper headlines), others (depending on the learner's cultural background) may not be so culture bound. Familiarity with subject helps understanding.
Linguistic knowledge	How much linguistic knowledge does the learner have? (i.e. knowledge of the systems and structures of English, not necessarily the ability to mobilise this knowledge). What linguistic knowledge is assumed by the task?	Some tasks may assume a certain amount of linguistic knowledge on the part of the learner, particularly those which have a grammatical focus, e.g. a written exercise requiring the learner to identify or manipulate certain grammatical structures.

⟫→

2 Task factors	Questions to consider	Comments/Examples
Relevance	Is the task relevant and meaningful to the learner?	Needs analysis can determine the areas in which learners want and need to operate. (For sample procedures see Brindley 1984; Nunan 1985a.)
Complexity	How many steps are involved in the task? How complex are the instructions? What cognitive demands does the task make on the learner? How much information is the learner expected to process in performing the task?	It seems reasonable to assume that learners move from being able to perform short, manageable tasks to longer and more complex ones, e.g. from recognising only key words in a text to understanding details.
Amount of context provided prior to task	How much prior knowledge of the world, the situation or the cultural context is assumed in the way the task is framed? How much preliminary activity is allowed for to introduce the task and set the context?	As proficiency develops, reliance on context seems to lessen, e.g. at beginning stages, learners often need to see a person speaking to understand, but they later develop the ability to understand without the help of context (e.g. telephone conversations).
Processibility of language of the task	Is the language that learners are expected to produce in line with their processing capacity?	Recent research into psycholinguistic processing constraints in second language acquisition

2 *Task factors*	*Questions to consider*	*Comments/Examples*
		(Pienemann 1985; Johnston 1985) gives an indication of syntactic structures which learners might be expected to produce at different developmental stages.
Amount of help available to the learner	How much assistance can the learner get from the teacher, other learners, books or other learning aids? In the case of interactive tasks, is the interlocutor sympathetic? Does s/he provide help? What is his/her tolerance level to non-standard language?	At beginning stages, learners may require more help, e.g. in conversation, the interlocutor may have to supply words and interpret learners' utterances.
Degree of grammatical accuracy/contextual appropriacy	How 'standard' does the task require learners to be? What is the desired 'effect on the interlocutor'? Does s/he expect or demand accuracy?	Different types of tasks may require greater or lesser degrees of accuracy, e.g. giving detailed instructions would probably require greater accuracy than an everyday exchange of personal information.
Time available	How long does the learner have to carry out the task.	'Time on task' has been shown to be a highly significant factor in learning.

⯈⯈→

3 Text factors	Questions to consider	Comments/Examples
Size and density of text	How long is the text? How much information does it contain? How concentrated is the information? How much repetition/recycling of the information is allowed for? In spoken text, how fast is the speech rate? In written texts, how dense/complex is the structure of the text? How clearly are the main ideas expressed?	Density and complexity of texts may be reflected in such factors as length of chunks to be processed, complexity of utterances (e.g. number of coordinate and subordinate clauses), amount of specialised vocabulary, etc.
Presentation/ format of text	How is the text presented in terms of layout/format? Is the format appropriate to the text type? What is the quality of print/recording?	Presentation of text can significantly affect learner performance, e.g. amount of background noise on recorded material affects learner comprehension. Use of 'authentic' format can also influence learner performance (e.g. use of newspaper cuttings rather than typed versions).
Contextual clues	Does the text contain non-linguistic clues which support meaning?	Presence of extra-linguistic clues (e.g. photos, drawings, sound effects, etc.) can significantly affect learner performance, e.g. a listening activity supported by video is probably easier than

3 Text factors	Questions to consider	Comments/Examples
		one in which an audio recording is used.
Content of text	What is the subject matter of the text? How abstract/concrete is it in relation to learners' experience? Is the information organised in a logical sequence?	Content familiarity has been shown to assist learners to process information.

An alternative suggestion to the sequencing problem is made by Corbel. This is to sequence input according to the logic dictated by a sequence of linked actions. This action-sequence approach has four steps:

1 Identify the learners' areas of interest and need in broad thematic terms.
2 Identify a series of communication situations related to that theme and link them to form an action sequence.
3 Select or devise materials appropriate to the situations in the action sequence.
4 Choose language points to focus on from the materials.

(Corbel 1985:74)

Corbel illustrates the action sequence approach as in Table 5.5:

⟫→

TABLE 5.5

Action sequence	Description	Teaching points example
1 A person arrives at a party.	Meeting strangers Introductions First names	I'm Ron. He's Ken. She's Sandra.
2 She is introduced to others by the host.	Socialising Introductions Offering Accepting/Declining Days of the week	This is my wife. Would you like a drink?
3 She and the hostess discuss the absence of the guest of honour.	Socialising Location The time	Where's Terry? Is Judy here? At work. At the pub.
Meanwhile–		
4 The guest of honour has been stopped by the police.	Giving personal information to officials Family names Asking for repetition Alphabet/Spelling	What's your family name? What is it again?
5 The person talks to others at the party.	Socialising Nationality Correcting Months	Where are you from? No, I'm from Ireland.
6 Meanwhile the guest of honour is still talking to the police.	Giving personal information to officials Address Checking Correcting Dates	What's your address? Is that seventy? No, seventeen. What's your date of birth?
7 The person talks to others at the party.	Socialising Identity	Who's that? Who are they?
8 Finally the guest of honour arrives.	Surprise/Relief Socialising Warning	Be careful! Don't drop it!

(op cit.:78)

At present, there is little empirical evidence to guide our decision making on task difficulty. Such decisions will therefore be largely intuitive and subjective. Unfortunately, such intuitive decision making is not always particularly reliable. To complicate matters, not all factors will have an equal bearing on determining task difficulty or complexity with all learners. Some will be relatively efficient in bringing their background knowledge to bear in comprehending a given message, other will rely more on their knowledge of syntax and lexis. Despite these difficulties, the curriculum designer has to make decisions about what will be taught early in a course and what will be taught later. Subjective decisions will need to be made, based on the factors listed above, and programmes will need to be trialled and revised in the light of experience. It would seem that, for the foreseeable future at least, the grading of communication tasks in a communicative curriculum will be largely intuitive.

5.6 Conclusion

In this chapter, we have examined some of the factors which need to be taken into consideration in the selection and grading of content. A procedure is described for deriving course content from an analysis of learner data. It has been argued that the specification of language goals is an important component of a learner-centred curriculum, particularly when such goals are couched in terms that learners understand, because they will then convey to learners important messages about learning processes. One argument commonly advanced against the involvement of the learner in the selection of content is that learners themselves are incapable of articulating needs. However, one group of teachers who have had considerable experience in learner-centred curriculum development have found that:

> At the 1+ (Intermediate) level most learners can state their needs reasonably clearly if given the right opportunity. I'm convinced that if learners feel that you have listened sympathetically to their perceived needs and discussed your views of the situation with them then they have a far more committed and active role in the learning process – they are, in fact, in control of their own learning, particularly if the consultation process is ongoing.
>
> (Brink *et al* 1985:9)

6 *Methodology*

6.1 Introduction

Traditional approaches to language teaching have tended to separate considerations of syllabus design from methodology. Broadly speaking, syllabuses specify the 'what' of teaching whereas methodology specifies the 'how'. Applied linguists, particularly those working within the British and European tradition, have tended to focus on syllabus design, whereas teachers, who are more concerned with the day-to-day aspects of teaching, have tended to be more interested in methodological considerations.

In recent times, the shortcomings of this lack of integration have become apparent, and there have been calls for a more integrated approach to language curriculum development and course design by applied linguists such as Richards (1984), Long (1985) and Nunan (1985a). In his proposal for an integrated approach, Nunan suggests that:

> Traditional models tend to restrict themselves to objectives specification, content selection, grading and evaluation. It is felt by some syllabus designers that there ought to be a rigid separation between syllabus design and methodology, in other words, that considerations of what to teach ought to be kept separate from how to teach. Such a separation has led in the past to such aberrations as the teaching of courses whose input was specified in functional–notional terms through an audiolingual methodology.
>
> In the model proposed here, all the elements are in interaction and each may influence the other. Objectives may be modified, altered or added to during the teaching–learning process. Decisions about what goes on in the classroom will be influenced, not only by pre-specified objectives, materials and activities, but also by needs, constraints (what is feasible, say, in the learning mode and environment) and by the evaluation feedback which emerges during the course itself.
>
> (Nunan 1985a:2–3)

This change in perspective has been prompted more by the development of communicative language teaching than anything else. While the rise of functional–notionalism prompted a widening of the content base, it was realised that for communicative language teaching to become a reality, there was a need for methodologies to reflect curriculum goals.

Another more recent impetus for change has been the development of classroom based acquisition studies. These are reviewed in some detail in the body of this chapter, and their practical implications are discussed.

In a recent dictionary of applied linguistics, methodology is defined as 'the study of the practices and procedures used in teaching, and the principles and beliefs that underlie them'. Methodology is said to include the following:

> (*a*) study of the nature of language skills (e.g. reading, writing, speaking, listening) and procedures for teaching them
> (*b*) study of the preparation of lesson plans, materials, and textbooks for teaching language skills
> (*c*) the evaluation and comparison of language teaching methods (e.g. the audiolingual method)
>
> (Richards, Platt and Weber 1985:177)

Richards and Rodgers (1986) define methodology in terms of approach (which provides theories on the nature of language and learning), design (specifying objectives, learning–teaching activities, learner and teacher roles, and the role of instructional materials) and procedure (dealing with classroom techniques and procedures).

Most teachers tend to think of methodology in terms of one or other of the '-isms' which are described in most general teaching texts. These include situational, audiolingual and communicative language teaching, as well as the 'fringe' methods such as Total Physical Response, Silent Way, Community Language Learning, the Natural Approach and Suggestopedia. These methods are analysed by Richards and Rodgers (1986) in terms of the approach/design/procedure framework, where the 'fringe' methods perhaps attract more attention than they deserve.

Here, we shall be looking at methodology from a communicative perspective, and the focus is upon learning and teaching activities which are consonant with this view.

Also to be examined is a central dilemma for those who subscribe both to communicative language teaching and to the learner-centred philosophy outlined in Chapter 3. It was suggested there that all aspects of the curriculum process, including methodology, be informed by data about and from the learner. However, research suggests that many adult learners are antipathetic towards classroom techniques and activities which can be broadly described as 'communicative'. In consequence, communicative language teachers who also subscribe to a learner-centred philosophy, find themselves on the horns of a dilemma when confronted by learners who have 'traditional' attitudes and beliefs about what are appropriate classroom activities. It is suggested that the way out of this dilemma must lie in extensive consultation, negotiation and information exchange between the teacher and the learners. This is confirmed in the empirical study which forms the basis for much of the final chapter of this book.

6.2   Methodology and Communicative Language Teaching

In Chapter 5 a procedure was outlined for using learner goals and communicative tasks as the point of departure for curriculum design. In that chapter, a distinction was drawn between real-world tasks and pedagogic tasks. One of the central issues which needs to be dealt with by curriculum designers who use tasks as the basis for selecting content and developing learning activities is that of transfer of learning. A basic assumption is that learners will be able to transfer knowledge and skills developed in the rather artificial environment of the classroom to new contexts and situations in the real world outside (Nunan 1988).

Assumptions about learning transfer have not always been borne out in practice. One of the major reasons for widening the scope of language content beyond grammatical structures, lexis and pronunciation, to functions, notions, settings and so on, was the fact that most learners seemed relatively inefficient at applying their grammatical knowledge to communicative language use outside the classroom.

The same thing happened with methodology. The assumption that grammatical paradigms, which had been internalised through various forms of classroom drill, could be put to communicative effect outside the classroom, seemed overly optimistic. The transfer of skills from the classroom context to other contexts did not occur as readily as was hoped. The result has been the development of activities which are meant to approximate in the classroom what happens in genuine communication outside. Teachers are exhorted to develop information-gap activities, and one- and two-way tasks in which learners must negotiate with each other to redress imbalances in the distribution of knowledge. Thus, in addition to the various drills and controlled language practice designed to develop accuracy, we have the whole panoply of communicative activities, including games, simulations and role plays which are meant to foster fluency.

In the communicative view of language which was described in detail in Chapter 3, language learning was characterised as a process of developing the ability to do things with language (as opposed to learning about language). In fact, there is not one but a cluster of approaches which parade under the general label 'communicative', all of which characterise language learning as the development of communication skills. Recent approaches recognise the limitations of language transfer, and suggest that at some stage learners should be encouraged to engage in class in some of the behaviours they will be required to use outside. While part-skills practice might involve some non-communicative activities such as drills, learners will also be expected to engage in substantial whole-skill practice.

Needless to say, it is not possible to simulate all behaviours in class. Neither is it necessary if we assume that some transfer will take place. Yet to be determined are the classroom tasks and activities most likely to facilitate skills transfer to the real world. The key questions which need to be determined by empirical research are:

To what extent does the ability to perform Task X in class correlate with the ability to perform Task X in real communication beyond the classroom?; and

To what extent does the ability to perform Task X in class correlate with the ability to perform Task Y and Z in real communication beyond the classroom?

In the traditional ends–means (or objectives–methodology) model, class-room activities are tied to performance objectives in a one-to-one relationship. However, as already intimated, such a relationship is neither necessary nor always desirable. It has been suggested that:

> ... there is no reason why rehearsing the final performance is necessarily the only or even the best way of reaching the [stated] goal. Indeed, there may be very good reasons for not spending a great deal of class time in actually carrying out terminal tasks related to performance objectives.
>
> (Nunan 1985a:15)

However, to reiterate, some real-world tasks will be rehearsed in class. Until we have firm evidence on the relationship between classroom learn-ing and non-classroom communication, between pedagogic tasks and real-world tasks, classroom teachers and instructional designers will have to rely on judgement, experience and intuition, even though these have not always served the profession particularly well in the past.

Some proponents of communicative methodologies see the prior specification of objectives as redundant, believing that any classroom activities which engage the learner in any sort of communicative language use will provide the necessary and sufficient conditions for learning (see for example Krashen and Terrell 1983). However, such a belief would seem to rest on the now largely discredited 'unitary competence hypothesis' (Oller 1979). What happens in class should relate, in some principled way, to what was planned to happen, even though it is unlikely that there will ever be a neat one-to-one relationship between intention and reality.

There have also appeared in the methodology market place comprehension-based communicative methodologies which have as their central article of faith the belief that comprehension is both necessary and sufficient for successful second-language acquisition (see for example Winitz 1981). Some of these also claim the empirical support which is so notably absent from most other methods. Asher (1977), for instance, claims that experimental students following his comprehension-based Total Physical Response method significantly out-perform control students in regular classes. Such claims, however, have to be treated with a good deal of caution, as there are suggestions that the post-treatment tests were by no means programme-fair:

> Asher (1972) and Asher, Kusudo and de la Torre (1974) investigated the effect of the Total Physical Response (TPR) method compared with a 'regular' programme. In the 1972 report, one of the stories used in classroom training in the TPR group is presented as an example; it is entitled 'Mr. Schmidt goes to the office'. Later in the report, we are informed that one of the criterion measures used to compare experimental (TPR) and control (regular) groups is a listening test involving a 'story entitled "Mr. Schmidt goes to the office"'(p. 136). In view of this, it is hardly astonishing that the experimental students dramatically out-performed controls (p = .0005). (On a reading test, no significant differences were found.)
>
> (Beretta 1986b:432)

In addition, there is research which suggests that learners need the opportunity for both comprehensible input and output (Long 1981; Nicholas 1985).

One criticism which could be levelled at a methodology in which real-world communication tasks are taken as the point of departure is that it will enable learners to do only the sorts of things which have been specifically taught in class; that such a methodology will not facilitate transfer of learning; and that it will, in effect, be a form of training rather than education. We saw in Chapter 4 that such a criticism is made by Widdowson in his critique of narrow-band ESP courses. He suggests that courses which aim to teach learners to carry out pre-specified tasks will produce speakers who are incapable of transferring that training to carrying out communication tasks which have not been pre-specified. General Purpose English courses (whatever these might be), on the other hand, will aim at the development of generalised and transferable communicative competence (whatever that might be). He suggests that:

> ESP is essentially a training operation which seeks to provide learners with a restricted competence to enable them to cope with certain clearly-defined tasks. These tasks constitute the specific purposes which the ESP course is designed to meet. The course, therefore, makes direct reference to eventual aims. GPE, on the other hand, is essentially an educational operation which seeks to

> provide learners with a general capacity to enable them to cope
> with undefined eventualities in the future. Here, since there are no
> definite aims which can determine course content, there has to be
> recourse to intervening objectives formulated by pedagogic theory.
> These objectives represent the potential for later realisation and
> are, so to speak, the abstract projection of aims.
>
> (Widdowson 1983:6)

However, as has already been pointed out, the degree to which courses
of one type or another do or do not equip the learner to react appropriately in situations which have not been specified in advance is a matter
for empirical investigation rather than speculation. Until such evidence
is forthcoming, it is not unreasonable to allow learners to practise in
class those skills which are directly relevant to the purposes for which
they have come to learn English in the first place. Certainly, until the
construct of 'general purpose English' has been more fully articulated,
verified by research, and operationalised, it would be well to develop
methodologies which are consonant with learners' communicative purposes.

6.3   Acquisition in the Classroom

It has been repeatedly suggested in these pages that we need to place
curriculum development on more secure empirical foundations. This is
no less true for methodology than for other curriculum elements. We
need methodologies which are psychologically and psycholinguistically
motivated, and which do not violate what we already know about language development. Unfortunately, much research has been either misleading or misused, leading to scepticism on the part of practitioners.
However, some promising avenues have opened up in the area of classroom-based acquisition research.

Second-language acquisition (SLA) has been a growth area in applied
linguistics research in recent years. A name commonly associated with
SLA is Stephen Krashen (1981, 1982). In fact, he is viewed by some
classroom practitioners as the high priest of the profession despite the
fact that comparatively little of his theoretical speculations are based on
his own empirical research, and that his practical suggestions are either
self-evident (make learning 'interesting'), or are based on unreasonable
extrapolations from such data as are currently available. However, he
has put SLA on the practitioner's agenda, and should be given credit for
that.

Krashen's Monitor Model suggests that there are two discrete
psycholinguistic processes operating in second-language development:

conscious learning and subconscious acquisition. According to the model, long-term language development occurs only through subconscious acquisition (or, to be more precise, that acquisition is central, while learning is peripheral to language development), and acquisition occurs when learners understand language which is a little beyond their current competence. A great deal of methodological speculation has been spawned by this comprehensible-input hypothesis.

The model further suggests that the classroom is one of the few places where comprehensible input is available to the learner. Such input is facilitated by the use of foreigner talk, by focusing on meaning rather than form, and by ensuring that the learners affective 'filter' is low.

In recent years, Krashen's work has been subjected to some searching criticism (see for example Gregg 1984; Johnston 1985; Pienemann 1985). These criticisms notwithstanding, second-language acquisition has developed as an important area of applied linguistics. The work of researchers such as Pienemann, Johnston, Ellis and Long, to name just a few, is of interest because it is based on data rather than speculation. There is by no means universal agreement by these researchers on the nature of the psycholinguistic processing operations underlying second-language acquisition. However, most share an interest in exploring the potential of the classroom as an environment where acquisition can be fostered.

Second-language acquisition research and its implications are of particular interest to practitioners who subscribe to the principles of communicative language teaching. Both focus on the development of meaning, and both recognise the importance of the negotiation of meaning as a stimulus to language development. Implicit in both is the belief that language development can occur through means other than sequential, step-by-step processing.

A central article of faith in Krashen's model is the belief that comprehension is the only factor necessary for successful language acquisition; the notion that speaking practice and the conscious learning of grammar are necessary is rejected. In support of his position he places a great of faith in the results of Asher's research.

> . . . those methods that provide more of the input necessary for acquisition, and that 'put grammar in its place' are superior to older approaches.
>
> (Krashen 1982:155)

In view of the questions surrounding Asher's empirical work, Krashen's comment is rather sanguine to say the least.

An alternative to the comprehensible-input hypothesis is the 'comprehensible-output' hypothesis, which stresses the importance of giving learners the opportunity of practising the target language (Swain 1985). It has been further suggested that learners need not only the opportunity of producing the target language, but that they also need the opportunity of being able to 'negotiate the new input, thereby ensuring that the language which is heard is modified to exactly the level of comprehensibility they can manage' (Long and Porter 1985). The negotiation of meaning through speech modifications and conversational adjustments is justified as follows:

> . . . if it can be shown that linguistic and/or conversational adjustments promote comprehensibility, and that comprehensibility promotes acquisition, it can be deduced that the adjustments promote acquisition.
>
> (Long 1985)

Long and Porter suggest that small-group work in the language classroom provides the optimum environment for negotiated comprehensible output. In fact, validity is claimed for group work on both pedagogical and psycholinguistic grounds. Pedagogical arguments include the following:

Group work increases the opportunities for learners to use the language.
Group work improves the quality of student talk.
Group work allows greater potential for the individualisation of instruction.
Group work promotes a positive affective climate.
Group work has been found to increase student motivation.

In providing a psycholinguistic rationale for group work, Long and Porter cite both Krashen's comprehensible-input and Swain's comprehensible-output hypotheses. Group work provides an environment in which learners can comprehend, it gives them opportunities for production and it provides contexts within which meaning can be negotiated.

Long and Porter also cite the second-language acquisition research on foreigner talk. Such talk consists of language in which syntax and interaction patterns have been modified. These modifications increase the amount of comprehensible input to which the learners are exposed, which, it is hypothesised, increases the rate at which they learn.

A number of classroom studies have also demonstrated other benefits from interactions between second-language learners. Porter (1985) was able to demonstrate that learners actually talked more in pair work with other second-language learners than with native speakers, and that, contrary to expectation, learners did not appear to learn each other's errors to any significant extent. A study by Varonis and Gass (1983) demonstrated that there are advantages in arranging pair work between learners of different proficiency levels, that such unequal dyads result in more negotiation of meaning than either native speaker–non-native speaker interactions or interactions between learners of the same proficiency level. Research such as this is reassuring for teachers who do not have the relative luxury of homogeneous classes.

The literature on language acquisition is substantial, and it is impossible to deal adequately with the subject here. Interested readers are referred to Day (1985), Ellis (1985) and Hyltenstam and Pienemann (1985) for more comprehensive accounts of the field. Ellis, in particular, provides a readable synthesis of SLA theory and research.

6.4 Stimulating Classroom Acquisition

Long and Crookes (1986) have been experimenting with techniques for stimulating acquisition in the classroom. They have found that 'two-way tasks', in which two participants must share information in order to complete a task or solve a problem, are effective in stimulating the development of communication skills. In particular, such activities provide an environment for the development of fluency and the negotiation of meaning (postulated by Long to be an important activity for acquisition). They also stimulate learners to mobilise all their linguistic resources, and push their linguistic knowledge to the limit.

Learners also seem to be prompted to mobilise all their linguistic resources when teachers increase the number of referential rather than display questions they ask. (Referential questions are those to which the teacher does not have the answer.) Compare the two following extracts taken from the same class using the same materials (a picture sequence of 'an accident'). In the first extract the teacher asks display questions, while in the second she involves the learners by asking referential questions. The second extract is, communicatively, much richer than the first.

1

T: What's the name of this? What's the name? Not in Chinese.
Ss: Van. Van.
T: Van. What's in the back of the van?
Ss: Milk. milk.
T: A milk van.
S: Milk van.
T: What's this man? (Driver)
S: Driver.
T: The driver.
S: The driver.
T: The milkman.
S: Millman.
T: Milkman.
Ss: Milkman.
T: Where are they?
Ss: Where are they?

T: Where are they? Inside, outside?
S: Department.
T: Department?
S: Department store.
T: Mmm. Supermarket.

2
S: My mother is by bicycle. By bicycle, yes, many, many water.
T: She had an accident?
S: In China, my mother is a teacher, my father is a teacher. Oh, she go finish by bicycle, er, go to . . .
S: House?
S: No house, go to . . .
S: School?
S: No school. My mother . . .
T: Mmm
S: Go to her mother.
T: Oh, your grandmother.
S: Grandmother. On, yes, by bicycle, by bicycle, oh is, um, accident. (gestures)
T: In water?
S: In water, yeah.
T: In a river?
S: River, yeah, river. Oh, yes, um, dead.
Ss: Dead! Dead! Oh!
T: Dead? Your mother? (General consternation)

Long has proposed a task-based curriculum for ESL which is not dissimilar to the procedure outlined in Chapter 5. A task is defined as:

> . . . a piece of work undertaken for oneself or for others, freely, or for some reward . . . examples of tasks include painting a fence, dressing a child, filling out a form, buying a pair of shoes, making an airline reservation, borrowing a library book, taking a driving test, typing a letter, weighing a patient . . . In other words, by 'task' is meant the hundred and one things people do in everyday life, at work, at play, and in between.
>
> (Long 1985:89)

Long's task-based syllabus has been developed by Long and Crookes (1986). At first sight, their suggestions look to be no different from the 'general communicative approaches' based largely on information-gap and problem-solving tasks. Underlying these approaches, however, is an assumption that the specific nature of the task and the content on which it is based are unimportant, that, as long as learners are productively engaged in a task, they will be acquiring the target language. In other words, these approaches seem to rest on what looks suspiciously like the unitary-competence hypothesis which asserts that there is a single language construct underlying all language ability, and that the development of skills in one domain will transfer maximally to all other domains.

This hypothesis has now been discredited, and it is generally accepted that skills transfer is likely to be more restricted than was previously thought. Recognition of this fact has been one reason for the development of learner-centred approaches to curriculum design.

Long's approach, however, does not rest on any notion of unitary competence. Rather, he tries to develop principles in which pedagogic tasks are systematically related to real-world tasks. He thus stresses the importance of basing classroom tasks on the prior identification of learner needs, and it can be seen from the following steps and examples how close his curriculum model is to the one proposed here. (His 'target tasks' and 'type tasks' are similar to the learner goals which are the point of departure for content specification as set out in Chapter 5.)

Long and Crookes propose the following steps:

1 Use learner needs identification to identify target tasks.
2 Classify target tasks into task types.
3 From task types, derive pedagogical tasks (second-language acquisition opportunities).
4 Sequence pedagogical tasks to form task syllabuses.
5 Evaluate achievement using task-based criterion-referenced tests.

The distinction between types of task is exemplified in Table 6.1:

TABLE 6.1

Target tasks	Task type	Pedagogical tasks
Buying/Selling bus, train, airline and theatre tickets	Buying/Selling tickets	Matching dialogue excerpts 1-way input/L Matching requests with ticket availability 1-way input/L Informing customer of seat availability 2-way/PW

Key
L: lockstep
PW: pair work

There still remains a great deal of empirical work to be done, particularly in terms of establishing difficulty levels for task types and in establishing the degree of learning transfer from one task type to another. However, at this stage, the methodological implications of task syllabuses look promising in that they attempt to integrate insights from classroom-acquisition research and principles of learner-centred curriculum design.

So far, it has been suggested that a task-oriented communicative curriculum will develop a methodology which takes the learner towards the classroom rehearsal of tasks and skills needed for communicating outside the classroom. Acquisition studies suggest that classroom communication can foster language acquisition, particularly if learners are given opportunities for productive language use and the negotiation of meaning in small-group work. This research also suggests that sequential, step-by-step learning, in which tasks and skills are carefully built up from simple to complex, can be supplemented by whole task activities in which a variety of skills are integrated.

Various task types have been developed to stimulate genuine whole-task practice in the classroom. These include information-gap tasks, language games, simulations and so on. While such tasks have their place in the communicative classroom, they do not always stimulate enthusiastic learner participation, nor is their relevance to the real world always apparent.

One activity which can be used to simulate the sorts of communication tasks which learners will be required to perform in the real world is role play. Richards presents a rationale for the use of role play, along with practical suggestions as to how role play can be utilised in class. He suggests that collaborative communication activities such as group work, problem-solving tasks, role plays and simulations exhibit the following characteristics:

> They provide opportunities to practice strategies for opening, developing, and terminating conversational encounters.
> They require learners to develop meanings collaboratively.
> They necessitate the use of turn-taking rules.
> They practice use of conversational routines and expressions.
> They involve learners in different kinds of roles, necessitating use of different styles of speaking.
> They require negotiated completion of tasks.
> They involve information sharing.
> They focus on comprehensible and meaningful input and output.
> They require a high degree of learner participation.
>
> (Richards 1985b:83)

The procedure described by Richards for utilising role play with intermediate learners is as follows:

> 1 Learners participate in a preliminary activity in which the topic and situation are introduced.
> 2 They then work through a model dialogue on a related topic which provides examples of the type of language which will be required.
> 3 Assisted by role cards, learners perform the role play.

〉〉〉→

4 Learners listen to recordings of native speakers performing the role play with the same role cards.
5 Follow-up activities exploit the native-speaker performance.
6 The entire sequence is then repeated with a second transaction on the same topic.

(*op cit.*:87–88)

By selecting topics and settings from the information obtained from learners through needs analysis, the classroom role plays can be made relevant to the perceived needs of the learners.

The most interesting suggestion in the Richards procedure is the use of native-speaker versions of the role plays. These act as 'master performer' models for the learners.

6.5   Methodology in a Learner-Centred Curriculum

It has thus far been argued that a communicative curriculum will use as its basic building block pedagogic tasks which, while they might not necessarily replicate, will be linked in principled ways to the real-world tasks learners might be required to engage in outside the classroom. It has also been suggested that classroom-based acquisition studies might provide psycholinguistically-motivated learning tasks. While accuracy-based activities such as drills and controlled practice will not be proscribed, prominence will be given to activities which promote fluency. Further, it would seem that small groups are probably the most effective way of grouping learners for communicative language work. Performance-based activities such as role play will also be promoted. These suggestions would seem to be supported by both pedagogical and psycholinguistic research.

So far, however, the most important actor in the drama, the language learner, has been left standing in the wings. In a learner-centred curriculum, methodology, as much as any other element in the curriculum, must be informed by the attitudes of the learners. What, then, do learners think are legitimate learning activities, and how do these compare with the perceptions of the teachers who instruct them?

In this section we shall attempt to answer this question by examining a number of studies which explore the perceptions of teachers and learners. While these studies do not directly compare teachers and learners, they provide the background for a study which does.

Background

Eltis and Low (1985), in a national survey of teaching processes within the Adult Migrant Education Program, questioned 445 teachers on the usefulness of various teaching activities. The rank ordering of these activities according to their perceived usefulness is set out in Table 6.2:

TABLE 6.2 RANK ORDERING OF TEACHING ACTIVITIES ACCORDING TO PERCEIVED USEFULNESS (ELTIS AND LOW 1985).

Activity	%
Students working in pairs / small groups	80
Role-play	56
Language games	51
Reading topical articles	48
Students making oral presentations	46
Cloze (gap filling) exercises	45
Using video materials	40
Student repeating teacher cue (drill)	34
Exercise in free writing	27
Setting and correction of homework	25
Listening and note-taking	25
Repeating and learning dialogues	20
Students reading aloud in class	21
Exercises in conference writing	18

Teachers were asked to choose the two activities which they found to be most valuable in their teaching. The activities which were rated as significant were:

– students working in pairs / small groups
– language games
– role play
– reading topical articles
– close (gap-filling) exercises.

In general, the Eltis and Low study supports the communicative language teaching study reported in Chapter 3. Both studies indicate that the teachers investigated favour activities and tasks which can be broadly typified as 'communicative'.

Alcorso and Kalantzis (1985) studied the perceptions of students. While they did not canvass exactly the same activities as Eltis and Low, there are enough similarities in the survey instruments to make comparisons. Their findings on the most useful parts of lessons according to a representative group of learners are set out in Table 6.3.

TABLE 6.3 MOST USEFUL PARTS OF LESSON ACCORDING
TO STUDENTS (ALCORSO AND KALANTZIS 1985).

Activity	%
Grammar exercises	40
Structured class discussion/conversation	35
Copying written material, memorising, drill and repetition work	25
Listening activities using cassettes	20
Reading books and newspapers	15
Writing stories, poems, descriptions	12
Drama, role-play, songs, language games	12
Using audio-visuals, TV, video	11
Communication tasks, problem-solving	10
Excursions with the class	7

Data from the Eltis and Low and Alcorso and Kalantzis studies indicate that while those teachers surveyed seem to rate 'communicative' type activities highly, learners favour more 'traditional' learning activities, the one exception being 'structured conversation'. In follow-up interviews with learners who took part in the survey, Alcorso and Kalantzis (1985) report that:

> There seemed to be a common view about the importance of grammar across respondents with different levels of English and from diverse educational backgrounds . . . In explaining their preferences, the learners said they saw grammar-specific exercises as the most basic and essential part of learning a language.
>
> (p.43)

> . . . conversation was another frequently mentioned activity considered useful for learning English . . . Typically what people meant by the word 'conversation' was speaking with the teacher, group and class discussions and question and and answer sessions with the teacher.
>
> (p.44)

> These activities [games, singing and dance] were among the most contentious since most students had firm views about their usefulness or uselessness. Again the divergence of opinion seemed to relate to people's educational background and socio-economic position. The most common comment from high-school or tertiary-educated migrants was that, in general, dance, singing and games were a waste of time.
>
> (p.48)

In a major study of the learning styles of adult ESL students, Willing (1985) investigated the learning preferences of 517 learners. His survey instrument contained 30 questions relating to class activities, teacher behaviour, learning group, aspects of language, sensory-modality options, and 'outside-class' activities. Learners, who were provided with bilingual assistance where necessary, rated each of these on a four-point scale.

A factor analysis of the data revealed patterns of variation in the responses with evidence for the existence of four different learner types. These are as follows:

'Concrete' learners: These learners preferred learning by games, pictures, films and video, talking in pairs, learning through the use of cassette and going on excursions.

'Analytical' learners: These learners liked studying grammar, studying English books, studying alone, finding their own mistakes, having problems to work on, learning through reading newspapers.

'Communicative' learners: This group liked to learn by observing and listening to native speakers, talking to friends in English, watching TV in English, using English in shops etc., learning English words by hearing them and learning by conversations.

'Authority-oriented' learners: These students liked the teacher to explain everything, writing everything in a notebook, having their own textbook, learning to read, studying grammar and learning English words by seeing them.

Despite the variation, there were some activity types which rated very highly overall. These were pronunciation practice, explanations to the class, conversation practice, error correction and vocabulary development. Others receiving low or very low ratings included listening to or using cassettes, student self-discovery of errors, learning through pictures, films and video, pair work and language games.

As already indicated, studies such as those be Alcorso and Kalantzis and Eltis and Low, while providing interesting indications, are not directly comparable. In order to provide data on learner and teacher perceptions which could be directly compared, a study was conducted using a survey instrument based on ten of the most and least popular student learning activities from the Willing study.

The Study

Sixty teachers from the Adult Migrant Education Programme were asked to complete a questionnaire which required them to rate the following activities on a four-point scale according to their degree of importance:

- pronunciation practice
- explanations to class

»→

- conversation practice
- error correction
- vocabulary development
- listening to / using cassettes
- student self-discover of errors
- using pictures, film and video
- pair work
- language games.

Items were rated and scored in an identical fashion to the Willing study. A comparison was them made between the two sets of data.

Results

Results of the comparison are set out in Table 6.4:

TABLE 6.4 A COMPARISON OF STUDENT AND TEACHER RATINGS OF SELECTED LEARNING ACTIVITIES

Activity	Student	Teacher
Pronunciation practice	very high	medium
Explanations to class	very high	high
Conversation practice	very high	very high
Error correction	very high	low
Vocabulary development	very high	high
Listening to / using cassettes	low	medium high
Student self-discovery of errors	low	very high
Using pictures/films/video	low	low medium
Pair work	low	very high
Language games	very low	low

These results indicate that only in one instance is there a match between the ratings of students and teachers, that is, in the importance accorded to conversation practice. All other activities are mismatched, some dramatically so, in particular pronunciation practice, error correction, listening to / using cassettes, student self-discovery of error and pair work. The results are represented diagrammatically in Figure 6.1:

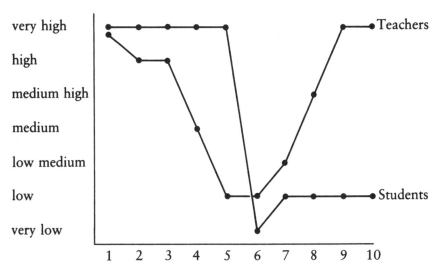

KEY
1. Conversation practice
2. Explanations to class
3. Vocabulary development
4. Pronunciation practice
5. Error correction

6. Language games
7. Using pictures/films/video
8. Listening to / using cassettes
9. Student self-discovery of errors
10. Pair work

FIGURE 6.1   TEACHER AND LEARNER RATINGS OF LEARNING ACTIVITIES: A
COMPARISON

Discussion

The data presented above reveal clear mismatches between learners' and teachers' views of language learning. The comparative study reported above demonstrates mismatches in all but one activity investigated, and quite significant mismatches in half of the activities. There is some difficulty in interpreting some of the Alcorso and Kalantzis and Eltis and Low data because of differences in the activities investigated. However, where comparisons are possible, mismatches are evident. Thus Alcorso and Kalantzis demonstrate that learners give a high rating to conversation practice and a low rating to the use of cassettes, audiovisuals, TV, video and language games. Eltis and Low confirm that teachers give a medium rating to the use of pictures, films and video, and a very high rating to pair work. The only area of conflict in the data occurs in the case of language games which received a high rating in the Eltis and Low study and a low rating in the comparative study.

Brindley (1984), in a series of interviews with teachers and learners, uncovered what seemed to be two mutually incompatible sets of beliefs about the nature of language and language learning by teachers and learners, and which would appear consistent with the studies reported on in the preceding section. He suggests that:

> It is clear that many learners do have rather fixed ideas (in some cases culturally determined) about what it is to be a learner and what it is to learn a language. These ideas, not always at a conscious level, run roughly thus:
> Learning consists of acquiring a body of knowledge.
> The teacher has this knowledge and the learner has not.
> The knowledge is available for revision and practice in a textbook or some other written form.
> It is the role of the teacher to impart this knowledge to the learner through such activities as explanation, writing and example. The learner will be given a programme in advance.
> Learning a language consists of learning the structural rules of the language and the vocabulary through such activities as memorisation, reading and writing.
>
> (*op cit.*:97)

The teachers' views, on the other hand, seemed to be as follows:

> Learning consists of acquiring organising principles through encountering experience.
> The teacher is a resource person who provides language input for the learner to work on.
> Language data is to be found everywhere – in the community and media as well as in textbooks.
> It is the role of the teacher to assist learners to become self-directing by providing access to language data through such activities as active listening, role play and interaction with native speakers.
> For learners, learning a language consists of forming hypotheses about the language input to which they will be exposed, these hypotheses being constantly modified in the direction of the target model.

These beliefs are reflected in the comments made on the sorts of learning activities preferred by learners. Teachers made comments such as the following:

> All they want is grammar.
> I tried to get them to watch a video, but they didn't like it.
> They didn't want to go on excursions. They wanted to stay in the classroom and do grammar exercises.
> They kept asking for a textbook.

Statements from learners seemed to confirm these views:

> Without the grammar, you can't learn the language.
> I don't want to clap and sing. I want to learn English.

I want something I can take home and study. We do a lot of speaking, but·we never see it written down.

(*op cit.*:96)

It would seem that differences between learners and teachers are to be accounted for in terms of the sociocultural background and previous learning experiences of the learners, and the influence on teachers of recent directions in communicative language learning and teaching. Such differences are likely to influence the effectiveness of teaching strategies and need to be taken into consideration in the development and application of teaching methodologies.

6.6   Negotiating Learning Activities

The data presented in the previous section, which have been taken from a number of different research studies, suggest that adult ESL learners may have fairly fixed ideas about which activities are appropriate for the classroom. Not all of these ideas are consistent with a communicative methodology, and there is evidence of conflict between the views of teachers and learners.

What happens, then, in the case of a teacher discovering that her students subscribe to 'traditional' rather than 'communicative' principles? It would seem that such a teacher, assuming she is committed both to a communicative methodology and also to a learner-centred philosophy, is in something of a dilemma. One the one hand, she could ignore the wishes of the learners and adopt a 'doctor knows best' attitude by insisting on communicative activities in the classroom which learners may not feel are valid. In so doing, she would be abandoning any hope of being learner-centred. On the other hand, she could abandon her communicative principles and allow the learners to engage in activities such as memorising grammar rules, which she may feel are not really assisting the learners to develop their communicative skills. (Of course, the dilemma is compounded by the fact that we simply do not, as yet, have conclusive empirical evidence one way or another on whether or not 'non-communicative' activities such as the learning of grammatical rules do or do not facilitate the development of communicative skills.)

There are, in fact, other alternatives. One could begin by setting traditional learning activities, and gradually try and move learners towards an acceptance of more communicative activities. The danger here is that the initial activities may inculcate a learning set which will be difficult to overcome later. For this reason, some teachers prefer to make their expectations quite clear from the beginning. Whatever choice is made, it would seem imperative to provide the maximum amount of information to learners, through bilingual assistance where necessary and/or possible, and to set up mechanisms to facilitate the maximum amount of negotiation and consultation.

However, this can create another problem which is that learners generally do not cast themselves in a consultative role. As Brindley discovered in his study of teachers and learners:

> The principle of consultation with learners is fundamental to a learner-centred system. However, many teachers expressed doubts regarding the feasibility of consultation, pointing out a number of potential obstacles: the conflicting ideas held by teachers and learners about their respective roles; the resultant problems of reconciling learner-perceived needs with teacher-perceived needs; the learners' inability to state their needs clearly.
>
> (Brindley 1984:95)

(See also the experience of 'Sally's' class in the case study reported in Chapter 10.)

These data would tend to reinforce one of the central themes developed here, that for learners to take part in curriculum processes, particularly for them to make informed choices on appropriate methodology, they need to be taught what it means to be a learner. The curriculum therefore needs to have dual aims, one set relating to the teaching of language, the other to the teaching of learning skills.

This becomes particularly crucial when mismatches such as those reported in the previous section occur. Somehow or other, the teacher who is committed to communicative language teaching needs to convince learners of the value of communicative activities.

In fact, it is not the case that learners are antipathetic to all communicative learning strategies. The Willing study (1985) revealed some interesting data on learner attitudes in this regard:

> It appears very strongly in the data that the general 'communicative' trend in language teaching has a highly-valued aspect, and also a considerably less-valued aspect, in the estimation of the majority of learners.
>
> 'Conversation in class', 'talking to friends', and 'learning by observing and interacting with Australians' were all rated very highly. In interviews and discussions it was clear that, in particular, methods which encourage 'real' conversational practice and discussion (with teacher intervention with suggestions and error correction) is the single most highly-valued learning modality.
>
> On the other hand, it appeared that what might be called the 'artificial' side of the communicative approach is relatively unpopular. Listening activities using cassettes; activities involving pictures, films and video; and (especially) 'games' all received quite low ratings.
>
> (Willing 1985:66)

6.7 Conclusion

If by 'real' conversational practice is meant learners being themselves and simulating in class the sorts of communicative activities which are required of them outside, it would seem that the sort of approach advocated here is validated by the data. Real-life and psycholinguistically-motivated pedagogic tasks seem to be both pedagogically and psycholinguistically sound, and also appear to have the general support of the learners themselves.

7 Resources for a Learner-Centred Curriculum

7.1 Introduction

At the classroom level, materials often seem more prominent than any other element in the curriculum. This no doubt is largely due to the fact that materials are the tangible manifestation of the curriculum in action. They are, in fact, omnipresent in the language classroom and it is difficult to imagine a class without books, pictures, filmstrips, realia, games and so on. Even the most austere classroom will have some sort of materials. The Community Language Learning class will have a tape recorder, while in the Silent Way class rods and charts will be the focus of attention. Inexperienced teachers very often look to materials first for assistance in planning their courses and also for teaching ideas. There is evidence that experienced teachers also look to materials when confronted with an unfamiliar class or learner type.

Materials are, in fact, an essential element within the curriculum, and do more than simply lubricate the wheels of learning. At their best, they provide concrete models of desirable classroom practice, they act as curriculum models, and at their very best they fulfil a teacher development role. Good materials also provide models for teachers to follow in developing their own materials.

Materials come in many shapes and formats. The most obvious distinction is between local materials produced by a teacher for her class, and those which are commercially produced. A survey conducted of several hundred teachers in one large ESL programme revealed that 73 per cent of teachers regularly used materials produced by themselves, while only 50 per cent used commercially-produced materials (Eltis and Low 1985).

Commercial materials may be complete, sequentially developed courses with teachers' books, students' books, audiotapes, filmstrips and photographs. One of the most comprehensive sets of materials, *Challenges*, contains all these components as well as films and videotapes. Many published materials are not sequential, but consist of discrete units which may supplement teacher-produced materials.

The advent of sophisticated, user-friendly computer packages such as those produced for the Apple Macintosh allow teachers to adapt commercial materials, or create their own, with a highly professional finish.

One of the problems with comprehensive, structured course materials, particularly those with a strong methodological bias, is that they can sometimes dictate what goes on in the classroom, leaving teachers with little opportunity to exercise their own creativity (although there is evidence that many teachers have an independent streak, and tend to modify materials to suit themselves).

7.2   Materials in a Learner-Centred Curriculum

Within a learner-centred system, experienced teachers report that they find certain sorts of materials more useful than others. In general, a range of materials which can be exploited in a variety of ways is more useful than a comprehensive package. As the focus will be on assisting learners to do in class what they will need to be able to do outside, the materials should reflect the outside world. In other words, they should have a degree of authenticity. This authenticity should relate to the text sources as well as to student activities and tasks. The materials should also foster independent learning by raising the consciousness of the learners and making them more aware of the learning process. This can be done in a variety of ways, such as building self-evaluation and assessment exercises into the materials themselves. Recognising the inevitability of mixed groups of learners (both in terms of proficiency and also in terms of preferred learning styles), materials should be designed so that they are capable of being used in a variety of ways and also at different proficiency levels. As already indicated, they should also be suggestive rather than definitive, acting as a model for teachers to develop their own variations. The materials should also reflect the sociocultural context within which they will be used.

Some of these characteristics will now be discussed in greater detail. The points which have been made are exemplified by some recently published materials which have been developed within a learner-centred context.

Authenticity

The concept of authenticity is one which has aroused a great deal of debate since it was first introduced. The term itself is open to a number of interpretations. The most commonly accepted one can probably be articulated as follows:

> 'Authentic' materials are usually defined as those which have been produced for purposes other than to teach language. They can be culled from many different sources: video clips, recordings of authentic interactions, extracts from television, radio and newspapers, signs, maps and charts, photographs and pictures,

timetables and schedules. These are just a few of the sources which have been tapped.

(Nunan 1985a:38)

Those who take a hard line on authenticity insist that these should not be edited in any way. However, teachers find that very often the quality of audio recordings is so poor (and the task, in any case, is so much more difficult than comprehending in face-to-face interactions) that these have to be re-recorded or simulated (Slade 1986).

Despite the difficulties associated with the use of authentic materials, they are justified on the grounds that specially scripted texts are artificial. The problem is that comprehending and manipulating scripted dialogues does not readily transfer to comprehending and using language in real communicative situations.

Just how different 'textbook' language is from real language can be seen in the following extracts. The first is a specially-written dialogue from a high quality coursebook, while the second is from a coursebook based on authentic interviews and conversations:

Interview with a Pop Star

Interviewer: First question, Chris. What makes you happy?
Chris: Seeing my records in the charts.
Interviewer: And what makes you sad?
Chris: Violence and poverty, war and suffering.
Interviewer: What was your most embarrassing moment?
Chris: When I missed the bus to my first concert.
Interviewer: What is your earliest memory?
Chris: A holiday in Spain with my parents and my sister when I was three and a half. We saw some fishermen.
Interviewer: What do you think of your fans?
Chris: I love them, don't you?
Interviewer: Who was your first girlfriend?
Chris: Which first girlfriend?
Interviewer: What would your ideal girl be like?
Chris: She would have blue eyes and long legs. She'd have a warm friendly personality and – she would have to like my mum.

(Candlin and Edelhoff 1982:128)

Pat is talking about jobs that her friends do.

Bronwyn: Tony wants to be a pilot – he's wanted – he's wanted to be a pilot – he's adopted – he's wanted to be a pilot ever since he came to me
Gary: mm
Bronwyn: he's never wavered from that
Pauline: mm

Pat:	a friend of mine, he was um . . .
Pauline:	well, I hope he gets it
Bronwyn:	mm
Pat:	he was doing oh – just joy-rides around the islands, flying all the people – he only has to work six months of the year
Bronwyn:	mm
Gary:	yes
Pat:	because that's all his contract is, six months a year but he gets such a high wage
Pauline:	yes
Bronwyn:	he has a holiday for six months (laugh)
Pat:	that he has a holiday for six months and um another ah guy Mark went to school with drives a speed boat from island to island, dropping passengers off here and there and everywhere
Bronwyn:	and they all get really good money
Gary:	they do
Pauline:	yes but it might get boring after a while
Bronwyn:	it does – you ask Helen

(Economou 1985:102)

While the written transcripts do not reveal differences in intonation and articulation, a cursory inspection reveals just how different they are in terms of syntax, discourse patterns and patterns of interaction. While non-authentic language has a place in the classroom, learners should not be denied the opportunity of exploring authentic language. Specially scripted dialogues and 'real' conversation are not mutually exclusive, as some might maintain; they simply have different pedagogical purposes in the classroom.

While authenticity is generally thought of in terms of the materials used in a given teaching activity (the materials might be radio or television advertisements, newspaper extracts, casual conversation, etc.), there are, in fact, other equally important types of authenticity. Candlin and Edelhoff suggest that there are at least four types of authenticity which are important for language learning and teaching. These are authenticity of goal, environment, text and task. In contrasting their view of authenticity with that of other coursebook writers, they assert that:

> Often writers of textbooks assume that it is enough if a few photographs or bits of newspaper extract are interspersed among sets of traditional language teaching exercises, not integrated or interrelated with them, but merely serving as a kind of veneer of Englishness to what is still a traditional book of drills . . . CHALLENGES offers an alternative to this and one which focuses on the authenticity of the tasks that the materials offer as possibilities to the learner and to the teacher.

(Candlin and Edelhoff 1982:9)

Another important type of authenticity (perhaps the most important of all) is what might be called 'learner authenticity'. By this is meant the realisation and acceptance by the learner of the authenticity of a given text, task, set of materials or learning activity. For learners to authenticate materials, these need, minimally, to fulfil two conditions. In the first place, they need to be recognised by learners as having a legitimate place in the language classroom. Secondly, they must engage the interests of the learner by relating to his interests, background knowledge and experience, and, through these, stimulate genuine communication.

The problem is that these two conditions can sometimes be mutually exclusive. In the studies of learners reported in the previous chapter, it was found that many learners come to the language class prepared only to legitimate such 'non-authentic' activities as drill and practice and the learning of grammatical rules and paradigms. One teacher found her learners rejected lessons based on extracts from television because they were not prepared to legitimate the use of television in the classroom.

In such cases, teachers have found a process of negotiation through which learners are gradually sensitised to a broader perspective on the nature of language and language learning is the most effective means of resolving conflict (see, for example, the case study in Chapter 9). In cases where materials and/or learning activities violate deeply-held or culturally-based beliefs, the materials should be abandoned.

An example of how learners can authenticate materials when their background knowledge is stimulated is presented in the preceding chapter where extracts from a lesson based on a picture sequence about an accident are presented. As soon as the teacher stopped asking display questions and started asking questions which prompted learners to activate their background knowledge learner language and interactions changed dramatically.

Levels of Difficulty

Traditionally, difficulty has been defined in linguistic terms, and levels of difficulty has been controlled for by controlling the difficulty of linguistic input to learners.

An alternative approach is to control the difficulty of the tasks required of the learners. Long contrasts difficulty, as traditionally determined, and difficulty as determined in his task-based syllabus design as follows:

> Grading is determined [in a task-based syllabus] by the degree of difficulty of the pedagogical tasks themselves (from simple to complex), as well as such normal considerations as variety, pace and duration. 'Difficulty', here, however, does not mean difficulty in terms of the linguistic demands of the full version of a given target task which indirectly motivated selection of a particular

pedagogic task. Rather, it refers to the difficulty of pedagogical tasks in such aspects as the number of steps involved in their execution, the number of parties involved, the assumptions they make about presupposed knowledge, the intellectual challenge they pose, their location (or not) in displaced time and space, and so on. Thus, of two pedagogic tasks involving one person selling another an airline ticket, the version in which the ticket was the last available would be ordered, all other things being equal, before a situation in which several options were open, e.g. between aisle and window seats, and in smoking and non-smoking sections.

(Long 1985:93)

(See also the discussion of task difficulty in Chapter 5.)

The example in Figure 7.1, taken from a listening comprehension course, demonstrates the setting of learning activities at different levels of difficulty within the one unit. This enables the course to be used with a class where the students are at different proficiency levels. Once again, the source texts are authentic.

FIGURE 7.1 TEXT: SHOPPING AROUND – GRACE BROS. ANNOUNCEMENTS

Announcement

'Customers, while you're in the store today, you could be the winner of ten thousand dollars worth of beautiful prizes from Philips and Grace Bros. For every Philips' electrical product that you purchase today, you receive an entry form in this beautiful Philips' competition. Ten thousand dollars worth of prizes, and you could be the winner. Full details are available right now from the small appliances department located on the ground floor of our homemaker store.'

Difficulty level 1

Where are the small electrical appliances in Grace Bros.?
Tick the right answer.
.... Second floor
.... First floor
.... Ground floor

Difficulty level 2

Tick the right answer.
There's a competition at Grace Bros. today.
If you're lucky, you could win $10
                       $1,000
                       $10,000   ⟫→

If you buy an electrical product, you can   enter the competition
                                                     enter the fashion store
                                                     win a ticket to the movies

To buy an electrical product, you go to   the fashion store
                                                     the homemaker store
                                                     the children's department

Difficulty level 3

Number the statements 1–6 according to the order in which they were made.
     'For every Philips' electrical product that you purchase today'
     'From the small appliances department located on the ground floor of our homemaker store'
     'You could be the winner of ten thousand dollars worth of beautiful prizes'
     'Customers, while you're in the store today'
     'Full details are available right now'
     'You receive an entry form in this beautiful Philips' competition'

(Jones and Moar 1985: 35–43)

In a professional development workshop for senior teachers involved in the selection and development of materials, participants were asked to select from a set of options the criteria they looked for in materials. The group (n = 27) were asked to rank a set of criteria from most to least important. Table 7.1 presents a composite ranking of criteria from most to least important.

TABLE 7.1 CRITERIA FOR SELECTING TEACHING MATERIALS FOR CLASSROOM USE

---

1 The materials make clear the link between the classroom and the wider world.
2 The materials foster independent learning.
3 The materials focus the learner on the learning process.
4 The materials are readily available.
5 The materials accord with the learners' expressed needs.
6 The materials can be used at more than one level of difficulty.
7 The pedagogical objectives of the materials are clear.

The ranking given by the group provides insights into their attitudes toward language teaching. The highest-ranking item, that the materials make clear the link between the classroom and the wider world, indicates adherence to the sort of utilitarian task-based approach to language teaching articulated in Chapter 3. Items 2 and 3 are also interesting in the light of data yielded by studies reported in other chapters. The desirability of fostering independent learning and of developing within learners skills of 'learning how to learn' are important characteristics in a learner-centred system. However, there is little evidence that these are being actively promoted at the classroom level. The fact that teachers recognise the need for resources for the development of learning skills is clearly articulated in the major study which forms the basis of the final chapter.

7.3   The Community as a Resource

A key aim of a learner-centred curriculum is to assist learners use the target language for communicative purposes outside the classroom. One of the justifications for using authentic materials is to generate classroom activities which simulate genuine communication in the classroom in the hope that this will facilitate transfer of learning.

No matter how carefully such simulations are developed, however, it is highly unlikely that conditions of communicative classroom use can be developed which replicate all aspects of communication outside the classroom. In order to maximise the potential of the classroom, it is necessary to develop student autonomy and meta-awareness. It is also important to encourage students to make links between classroom learning and outside language use, and to stimulate them to use the language as much as possible outside the classroom.

One obvious way of developing this focus outwards from the classroom to the community, is to encourage learner involvement in the community. Many teachers attempt to do this by taking students on excursions, bringing in guest speakers from the outside community and so on. The difficulty here is in convincing learners of the value of activities which take them outside the classroom. There is evidence that many learners do not rate the opportunity of engaging in outside activities such as excursions very highly (see for example Nunan 1986a). There is a feeling among these learners that excursions and similar activities are not valid language-learning activities. It is therefore important for the teacher to consult with learners, and to structure outside activities in such a way that the benefits are tangible and their relationship to the language-learning process is evident. This kind of involvement in the community is clearly only possible in situations where the community language is the target language, i.e. generally in ESL situations. But even in EFL situations opportunities may be found for bringing learners into contact with the target language in the wider community.

Obviously, some learner goals are easier than others to reconcile with an outside-oriented classroom. Vocationally-oriented courses, for instance, very often include work placement, and it is not unusual for students to rate these placement opportunities as the most valuable aspect of their language course. One such course is the Crossover Course, developed to improve learner proficiency in relation to the job-seeking process. Two teachers who co-ordinated this course described its aims as follows:

> The aims of the Crossover course were to develop communicative language competence by providing the opportunity for interaction and communication in a real life situation (i.e. work place) and by providing a context for extrapolating and discussing any communicative problems encountered, highlighting the language skills needed and developing appropriate strategies . . .
>
> (Burnett and Hitchen 1985:i)

In evaluating the Crossover course, the co-ordinators discovered that:

> . . . the course was very successful. There was a high degree of correlation between participants' expectations and the stated aims of the course, and the course met or surpassed their expectations.
>
> (*op cit.*:38)

Montgomery and Eisenstein, in an attempt to forge links between classroom language work and the use of language outside the classroom, developed an experimental oral communication course (OCC). The course was structured around a series of weekly field trips which took the learners out of the classroom to environments in which language had to be used for communication. Community sites were chosen on the basis of the expressed needs and interests of the learners. The excursions were related to classroom work through the following steps:

1 Students listen to a tape recording related to the focus for the week and complete listening comprehension exercises.
2 Students, in small groups, work through a variety of oral exercises.
3 These exercises lead into the development of a task related to the forthcoming field trip. (Tasks can include interviews, hypothesis testing, the gathering of evidence, etc.)
4 The field trip is undertaken. During the trip, learners encounter a range of natural language and engage in a question and answer session with a host from the site.
5 Students complete an evaluation sheet to determine how much they have understood.

6 In class, the questions and answers for the trip are reviewed. Follow-up activities include role plays, debates and 'the development of a plan of action to address a particular problem'.

(Montgomery and Eisenstein 1985:321)

The OCC was evaluated by comparing the students who took part in the programme with a control group of students taking part in a traditional ESL class. Students in the control and experimental groups were matched for proficiency, native language, length of time in the target country and socioeconomic status. All students were given an oral proficiency rating at the beginning and end of the course and were compared on accent, grammar, vocabulary, fluency and comprehension.

The results demonstrated gains by both groups, with the OCC group outscoring the control group on all measures. According to the researchers, the most interesting result was the fact that the area of strongest improvement for the experimental group in comparison with the control group was in grammatical accuracy. In commenting on this, they say:

> [The result] was surprising since there was no formal teaching of grammar in the OCC course and minimal error correction. One possible explanation is that the OCC programme enhanced the acquisition of English for the learners. Krashen (1978) defines acquisition as an unconscious process which occurs when the learner's focus is on meaning rather than on linguistic form, exactly the case for the OCC students. All students in the evaluation were exposed to a formal linguistic environment providing rule isolation and feedback. The data indicate for the OCC learners, however, a combination of form-oriented and meaning-oriented language teaching was more beneficial than form-oriented teaching alone. An experience such as that provided by the OCC may be particularly crucial for the development of grammatical accuracy in individuals who have little out-of-class contact with English.
>
> (*op cit.*:329)

The two experiments cited demonstrate that, when appropriately managed, building community-based learning experiences into a language course can lead to significant language gains. Such out-of-class experiences also seem to be highly regarded by most of the participating students. This result seems to conflict with other studies which demonstrate an aversion on the part of students to out-of-class activities. However, it may well be that the negative reactions have come from learners for whom few links have been made between in-class learning and out-of-class activities and with whom there was no attempt either to negotiate or rationalise the activities. In both of the experiments described here, such links were clearly made.

7.4   The Teacher as Developer of Resources

In this section, we shall look at a study set up to gain insights into the processes by which teachers transform teaching resources (the 'raw materials' of the classroom) into units of work.

Background

In recent years, the growth of classroom-based research has begun to provide us with more data on what teachers actually do in class, as opposed to what applied linguists and curriculum specialists say they ought to do (see for example Dinsmore 1985; Long and Sato 1983; Long and Crookes 1986; Nunan 1987). However, most of this research has focused more on aspects of classroom interaction than on programme planning and implementation. Other studies have focused on the teacher as methodologist (see for example Swaffar, Arens and Morgan 1982).

In general education, conventional wisdom has it that formal preparation, including post-graduate study, is perceived by teachers as being markedly inferior to classroom experience in professional development. Lawton, for instance, reports that:

> Students leaving college and entering schools are sometimes advised by practising teachers to 'forget all that theory and get on with the real teaching'.
>
> (Lawton 1973:7)

The following study was undertaken in order to gain insights into the processes by which teachers with varying degrees of experience transform materials into units of work.

The research question for the study was as follows:

What differences are discernible between teachers with different degrees of experience (as indicated by years of teaching experience) in transforming learning resources into a unit of work and in implementing the unit in the classroom?

Subjects

One way of setting up the study would have been to identify a group of TESOL teachers with a range of experience, give them a set of materials, and ask them to take part in a 'what if . . .' introspective study. 'What would you do with these materials if you had a class of X, Y and Z?' However, given the frequent misperceptions between what teachers think they do and what they actually do, it was felt desirable to have teachers plan and implement a unit of work with a real class. This meant identifying teachers working with students at the appropriate proficiency level for the materials (i.e. Initial Proficiency – Ingram 1984). In the event, 26 subjects were finally located who had students at this level and who were willing to take part in the study. Table 7.2 shows the breakdown of subjects into four groups according to years of experience.

TABLE 7.2 BREAKDOWN OF SUBJECTS
ACCORDING TO YEARS OF EXPERIENCE

Group	n	Years of experience
A	9	4–
B	7	4–6
C	5	6–8
D	5	8+

Procedure

Each teacher was provided with an authentic taped message and a set of worksheets. The materials were 'innovative' in that they were designed to teach listening skills, based on authentic sources, to low-level students. The teachers had not come across the materials before. Teachers were instructed to prepare and teach a unit of work (the term 'unit' rather than 'lesson' was used as it is less specific in terms of time) based on the materials to their regular class and to provide detailed information on the following:

- the aims of the unit
- the length of time it took to teach the unit (including the time allocated to different learner configurations)
- an indication of how the unit was introduced
- a description of the steps in the lesson
- a description of any changes that were made to the materials
- an evaluation of student reaction to the material
- an indication of intention to use similar materials in future
- an indication of the best features of the materials
- an indication of the least liked features of the materials
- an estimation of the suitability of the materials for the designated group.

Results

The data collected from the teachers are set out in Tables 7.3–7.12.

TABLE 7.3 STATED AIMS OF THE UNIT AS TAUGHT

Aims	Group A	B	C	D
Listening for gist	2	0	2	1
Vocabulary development	3	2	2	2
Identifying key words	1	1	1	1
Listening for specific information	6	2	2	1
Revision of previous language points	2	0	0	1
Developing fluency	0	1	0	0
Encouraging prediction	0	1	0	0
Promoting discussion	0	0	1	0
Developing function skills	0	0	0	1
Introducing theme 'shopping'	1	2	1	1
Developing listening skills	1	1	2	1

From Table 7.3 it can be seen that there is a large measure of agreement about appropriate aims for the materials. The 46 aims nominated by the teachers were collapsed into eleven groups, and of these, seven accounted for 34 of the responses. There is nothing in the data to suggest that responses from more experienced teachers cluster around aims which are different from those selected by inexperienced teachers.

TABLE 7.4 LENGTH OF UNIT AND STUDENT CONFIGURATION (IN MINUTES)

	Groups A mean	%	B mean	%	C mean	%	D mean	%
Teacher-fronted	40.6	41.2	34.2	42.7	76.0	70.3	105	64.0
Small-group	12.5	12.6	15.8	19.8	19.6	18.1	24.0	14.6
Pair-work	17.5	17.8	13.3	16.6	0	0	15.0	9.1
Individual	28.1	28.6	21.8	17.5	12.4	11.5	20.0	12.2
Total	98.75		80.0		108.0		164.0	

Table 7.4 provides the mean lengths of units, and also the amount of time taken for whole-class (teacher-fronted), small-group, pair and individualised work. Here, there does seem to be a pattern, with the more experienced teachers tending to get more out of the materials.

However, when the amount of time devoted to different learner grouping is examined, it can be seen that the amount of time spent by students in classes of less experienced teachers is more evenly distributed between the different possible configurations than was the case in classes taught by more experienced teachers. The more experienced teachers tended to spend the bulk of their time in teacher-fronted activities (70.3% and 64.00% respectively for the two most experienced groups). This could indicate that experienced teachers felt the materials, given their innovative nature, needed more teacher mediation, explanation and support.

TABLE 7.5 INTRODUCING THE UNIT OF WORK

	Group			
	A	B	C	D
Introduction of key vocabulary	5	3	0	0
General discussion of theme	1	0	2	3
Studying poster/picture	4	0	1	0
Starter (guessing/brainstorm, etc.)	1	2	3	1
Teacher explanation	1	3	1	0
Revision activity	1	1	0	1
No introductory activity	0	0	0	1

In terms of introductory activities, Table 7.5 shows that the less experienced teachers tended to use the more predictable activities of vocabulary introduction and picture contextualisation before introducing students to the materials themselves, while there was more variety in the activities developed by the more experienced teachers. The data are interesting in that they demonstrate a relative lack of attention to meta-activity (e.g. teacher explanation and revision activities) by all teachers.

TABLE 7.6 MEAN NUMBER OF STEPS IN THE UNIT

Group			
A	B	C	D
7	6	5	4.4

Table 7.6 shows the mean number of steps in the unit of work. There was a wealth of detail provided by teachers on the steps and activities in the unit of work which they developed. Unfortunately, there is no room to present these here. The table does show that as experience increased there is a decline in the number of activities undertaken. Taken with the data from Table 6.4, this indicates that, not only are more

experienced teachers better able to get more mileage out of a given set of materials, but that they are able to sustain activities for longer periods.

TABLE 7.7 CHANGES AND MODIFICATIONS TO MATERIALS

	Group			
	A	B	C	D
No modifications	4	4	2	2
Key word put on language master	1	1		
Use of department store poster	3			
Creation of pre-unit vocabulary activity	1	1		
Use of supplementary materials		2		2
Changed order of activities		1	1	
Simplified worksheets			1	
Changed some vocabulary items			1	1

From Table 7.7 it can be seen that almost half the teachers were satisfied with the materials as they stood and saw no need to make any modifications. One of the more experienced teachers indicated that she would have simplified the worksheets, while two other experienced teachers reported that they would have changed some of the vocabulary items if they were using the materials on a regular basis.

TABLE 7.8 STUDENT REACTION AS PERCEIVED BY TEACHERS

Group			
A	B	C	D
3.3	3.75	3.78	4.0

KEY
1=unfavourable
5=favourable

Table 7.8 shows student reaction as perceived by the teachers. Interpreting these second-order rating scales is always difficult, as one never knows how accurately the second party is reflecting the views of the first. From the data, there is a clear growth in the perceived approval ratings from least to most experienced teachers, with the most experienced teachers indicating the highest approval rating by students. However, it should not be inferred from this that more experienced teachers are able to make materials more interesting and relevant to their students, for the reason already given. It has been suggested that the data may indicate more confidence by experienced teachers in their own teaching (Burton personal communication).

TABLE 7.9 INTENTION TO USE SIMILAR MATERIALS IN FUTURE

| | Group | | | |
	A	B	C	D
Yes	8	7	5	5
No	1	0	0	0

From Table 7.9 it can be seen that only one of the 26 teachers taking part in the study did not intend to use similar materials in future, and additional comments made by the teachers were highly favourable. Combined with the data in Table 7.10, it would indicate that teachers were almost universally favourably disposed toward the use of authentic materials in class. This is interesting, given the resistance of many low-proficiency students to such materials.

TABLE 7.10 BEST LIKED FEATURES IN THE MATERIAL

| | Group | | | |
	A	B	C	D
Authenticity	6	5	4	3
Clear worksheets	1	2	2	
Attractive pictures/illustrations	4	2	2	3
Recycling vocabulary	1			
Selective listening activities	3	1		2
Cultural authenticity	2	1	1	1
Clear instructions		1	2	

TABLE 7.11 LEAST LIKED FEATURES IN THE MATERIAL

| | Group | | | |
	A	B	C	D
Background noise / tape quality	5	2	2	2
Irrelevant content, e.g. Sydney setting	2		2	
Too many handouts	1	1	2	
No preliminary chart	1			

⟫→

| | Group | | | |
	A	B	C	D
Unsuitable vocabulary	1	1		
Tape too fast and difficult	1	1	1	
No script available		1		
No clear demarcation between activities		1		
Need extensive preparation for 0+		1		
Too few tasks per activity				1
Need extension worksheets				2

Tables 7.10 and 7.11 were intended to elicit information from teachers on the good and bad features of the materials. Here there is a large measure of agreement about what was good about the materials but less agreement about the negative aspects. There seems to be no particular pattern differentiating experienced from inexperienced teachers.

TABLE 7.12 SUITABILITY FOR DESIGNATED PROFICIENCY LEVEL

| | Group | | | |
	A	B	C	D
Yes	7	5	4	5
No	2	2	1	0

Finally, from Table 7.12, it can be seen that there was general agreement about the suitability of the materials for the designated proficiency level, with only five teachers out of the 26 indicating that the materials were too difficult.

Discussion

It would be an error to read too much into what was essentially a preliminary investigation of the programme planning and implementation activities of teachers with varying degrees of experience. One of the major reasons for caution is the small sample size. A second is that it was impossible, given the nature of the study, to control for other subject variables such as formal TESOL training. Nevertheless, the investigation does tend to indicate that classroom experience may not, of itself, be a significant variable in professional development.

The implication for teacher training is that, in terms of materials development and exploitation, experience needs to be coupled with other aspects of professional development. ('Classroom experience is more than duration (endurance!); it is variety and intensity. Professional development programmes are about structuring and evaluating that experience.' Burton personal communication.) In addition to experience, teachers need the time, opportunity and support to reflect on that experience through a variety of professional development activities which should include professional development programmes, collegiate consultations and action research projects. This issue is taken up and developed in Chapter 9, and again in Chapter 10.

7.5 Conclusion

In a language programme committed to the direct development of the sorts of skills required by learners outside the classroom, it is of vital importance to create as many links as possible between what happens in the classroom and what happens outside.

In developing these links, resources for learning have a vital part to play. As far as possible, community resources should be exploited as a basis for the development of authentic classroom materials. Where appropriate, learning activities should also be developed which require the learners to practise their developing language skills in the community itself.

Whatever the attitude, however, materials, no matter how comprehensive, should never be seen as a panacea, nor should they be seen as substitutes for professional classroom practitioners. Experience from other areas has demonstrated time and time again that materials are only as good as the teachers who use them, and that the attempt to produce 'teacher proof' materials is both futile and undesirable.

8 *Assessment and Evaluation*

8.1 The Place of Evaluation in the Curriculum

No curriculum model would be complete without an evaluation component. While it is universally recognised as an essential part of any educational endeavour, it is the component about which most classroom practitioners generally claim the least knowledge, and is the one area of the curriculum about which many teachers express a lack of confidence. In this chapter it will be argued that in a learner-centred curriculum model both teachers and learners need to be involved in evaluation. It will also be argued that self-assessment by learners can be an important supplement to teacher assessment and that self-assessment provides one of the most effective means of developing both critical self-awareness of what it is to be a learner, and skills in learning how to learn.

Evaluation can, in fact, occur at various levels. At a macro-level national and state programmes can be evaluated. At this level evaluation will probably focus on administration and be carried out largely by personnel with evaluation expertise. Local, or centre-level, evaluation will be more circumscribed and involve administrators and teachers.

Micro-evaluation is conducted at the classroom level and involves teachers and learners.

Here we shall be principally concerned with evaluation at the micro-level, and the relatively informal evaluation techniques and procedures described in the latter part of this chapter are designed for use by teachers and learners at the classroom level.

As evaluation is intimately tied to the rest of the curriculum, it will be affected by changes to other curriculum elements. For example, any change to the goals and objectives of a given programme must be reflected in the evaluation procedures which are used within that programme. A vivid example of the way changes in goals and philosophies must also be reflected at the level of evaluation can be seen in relation to the development of communicative language teaching. Here, changes at the levels of syllabus design and methodology had a marked influence on evaluation as it was unsatisfactory to evaluate courses designed to improve students' communicative abilities by continuing to administer tests of linguistic knowledge.

This need for a change in focus has been voiced in the following way:

116

The distinction between usage and use is of great importance for teaching and testing. It implies that a test cannot be based on a selection of items chosen on linguistic grounds alone, and that to devise an effective test, it is necessary to specify how a testee requires to use the language. The criterion for success lies not in formal correctness but in communicative effectiveness ... Changing the emphasis from usage to use means also changing ideas concerning the specificity of tests. From the usage point of view, a language can be seen as a unified entity with fixed grammatical patterns and a core of commonly-used lexical items. Equipped with a mastery of these language patterns, it is hoped the user will learn to cope with the situations he finds himself in. Therefore, a single test of the learner's language proficiency based on formal usage should prove an adequate indication of ability to cope with real situations. But from the point of view of the role of language in communication, such a view is greatly over-simplified. Different patterns of communication will entail different configurations of language skill mastery, and therefore a different course or test content. From the use point of view, language loses its appearance of unity and must be taught and tested according to the specific needs of the learner.

(Carroll 1981:7–8)

Carroll has been quoted at some length because behind his statement are two important points. The first of these is that any evaluation or assessment procedure will be underpinned by views on the nature of language and language learning. These views need not be explicitly stated. The evaluator may not even be able to articulate them, but they will be there just the same. This point will re-emerge when we come to consider the construct validity of proficiency scales.

The second point worth noting is that, in communicative testing, the testing procedures should relate directly to the objectives of the course. In other words, they should aim to test what has been taught. This point is not as obvious as it might at first sight seem. In fact, a case can be made for relatively indirect means of assessment. Testing communicative skills directly can be a very awkward process; in some situations it may be almost impossible. If it can be shown that there is a high correlation between the ability to perform communicative tasks and performance on, say, a pencil and paper test of grammar, a case could be made for the use of grammar tests, which are much easier to administer and assess.

This, essentially, is the argument used by Oller (1979), who advocated the use of non-communicative tests such as cloze and dictation on the grounds that they correlated highly with other more communicative tests. However, there are a number of reasons why such an approach is unsatisfactory. In the first place, the construct, or concept, of language underlying Oller's work has not stood the test of time. Secondly, it is desirable, for a number of reasons, for a test to appear to test what has been taught, that is, it is desirable for the test to have high face validity. Finally, as assessment procedures inevitably seem to have a major influence on what happens in the classroom, it is desirable for these procedures to mirror what curriculum designers feel should be going on. The procedures, in Morrow's words, should have 'washback' validity (Morrow 1985).

8.2   Some Key Concepts in Evaluation

This section is devoted to an exploration and clarification of some key concepts, in particular, the concepts 'assessment' and 'evaluation'. These terms are often used interchangeably, when, in fact, they mean different things. Here, assessment is taken to refer to the set of processes by which we judge student learning. It is generally assumed that such learning has come about as the result of a course of instruction. Within the curiculum framework delineated here, the term refers to procedures for measuring the extent to which students have achieved the objectives of a course.

Evaluation, on the other hand, is a wider term, entailing assessment, but including other processes as well. These additional processes are designed to assist us in interpreting and acting on the results of our assessment. The data resulting from evaluation assist us in deciding whether a course needs to be modified or altered in any way so that objectives may be achieved more effectively. If certain learners are not achieving the goals and objectives set for a course, it is necessary to determine why this is so. We would also wish, as a result of evaluating a course, to have some idea about what measures might be taken to remedy any shortcomings. Evaluation, then, is not simply a process of obtaining information, it is also a decision-making process.

I am aware that this conceptualisation, which links assessment and evaluation to course goals and objectives, can be interpreted as a narrow ends–means one which may preclude the generation of insights and hypotheses about what is really going on in the curriculum process. (I am grateful to Alan Beretta (personal communication) for pointing this out to me.) However, the articulation of goals and assessment has particular value in a learner-centred curriculum, in which one set of goals will relate to the development of meta-cognitive skills on the part of learners. It is hypothesised here that making the intentions of the educational endeavour explicit to learners, and, where feasible, training them to set their own goals and assess their own learning outcomes, will make them better learners in the long run. In addition, I do not believe it is the case that a system in which, at some level, goals are related to outcomes, must necessarily be blind to unintended outcomes, nor that it must necessarily preclude illuminative forms of evaluation.

In mainstream education, the development of course goals and objectives has generally been seen as an important part of the process of assessment on the grounds that if we have not articulated what it is we want our learners to be able to do at the end of a course, it is difficult to judge whether we or they have succeeded or failed. Those who take this instrumental view argue that by articulating goals and also, ideally, performance objectives, we are in a much better position to judge the degree to which the assessed curriculum is consonant with the planned curriculum.

One evaluator who argues strongly for such a view is Gronlund, who offers the following definition:

> Evaluation may be defined as a systematic process of determining the extent to which instructional objectives are achieved by pupils. There are two important aspects of this definition. First, note that evaluation implies a systematic process, which omits casual, uncontrolled observation of pupils. Second, evaluation assumes that instructional objectives have been previously identified. Without previously determined objectives, it is difficult to judge clearly the nature and extent of pupil learning.
>
> (Gronlund 1981:5)

Gronlund is here using 'evaluation' in the sense in which I am using 'assessment'. However, he goes on to suggest that evaluation should involve both quantitative descriptions based on measurement and qualitative, non-measurement, descriptions. These data are used for making value judgements about the efficiency of a course of instruction.

It is important at this point to note that evaluation is not something which only takes place summatively, at the end of a course of instruction. Informal monitoring should, in fact, be happening right through the course.

Any element in the curriculum process may be evaluated, as any may affect learner progress, and it is up to individual teachers and curriculum personnel to decide how widely they should cast the net. Some obvious candidates for evaluation are initial planning procedures, programme goals and objectives, the selection and grading of content, materials and learning activities, teacher performance and the assessment processes itself as well as learner achievement. The evaluation of these different curriculum elements is considered in greater detail in 8.3.

The concepts of validity and reliability are crucial to assessment. Validity refers to the extent to which assessment procedures actually do what they were designed to do. Reliability refers to the consistency of assessment procedures. Tests, for instance, are of little use if they give different results each time they are administered. In addition, assessment procedures at the micro-level must be practical.

Of all these qualities, validity is probably the most complex and difficult to conceptualise as well as to achieve. There are various types of validity. Gronlund documents three of these, content validity, criterion-related validity and construct validity, in the manner shown in Table 8.1:

TABLE 8.1

Type	Meaning	Procedure
Content validity	How well the sample of tasks represents the domain of tasks to be measured	Compare the test tasks to the test specifications describing the task domain under consideration
Criterion related validity	How well test performance predicts future performance or estimates current performance on some valued measures other than the test itself	Compare test scores with another measure of performance obtained at a later date (for prediction) or with another measure of performance obtained concurrently (for estimating present status)
Construct validity	How test performance can be described psychologically	Experimentally determine what factors influence scores on the test

Of these, construct validity is the most problematic. This is because constructs are abstractions, pschological qualities which are assumed to underly various forms of observable human behaviour. The construct 'intelligence', for instance, can not be seen, but is inferred from the ability of individuals to solve various sorts of verbal, numerical and spatial problems. This creates a dilemma for the test constructor. What happens if results on a test do not bear out the predictions of the construct which is assumed to underly the test? Is the test at fault, or the construct, or both?

In the field of language testing there are many unresolved questions relating to the construct 'communicative skill'. Some of these questions are as follows:

Does the construct consist of a single psychological factor, or a number
of factors?
If it does consist of more than one factor, to what degree are these
separate, and to what degree are they related?
What are these factors?
How do they combine in communicative performance?
What sort of variation is there from one learner to another?

In order to answer these questions, work needs to proceed on two fronts.
On the one hand, we need empirical data on the development and use
of language for communication by both native speakers and second-language learners. On the other hand, we need adequate theoretical models
which account for the empirical data in the most parsimonious way
possible. Without such data and models, the development of satisfactory
tests of communicative performance is difficult, and the interpretation
of data yielded by such tests becomes almost impossible.

These issues will be discussed in greater detail when we come to
examine the construct validity of proficiency rating scales.

8.3   Some Key Questions in Evaluation

In this section a number of key questions relating to evaluation are
explored. These are the 'what', 'who', 'when' and 'how' questions. The
evaluator needs to consider which elements in the curriculum should be
evaluated, who should conduct the evaluation, when the evaluation
should take place, and by what means.

As indicated in 8.2, any element in the curriculum may be evaluated.
Some of the questions relating to each of these elements which an evaluation may wish to address are shown in Table 8.2:

TABLE 8.2

Curriculum area	Sample questions
The Planning Process Needs analysis	Are the needs analysis procedures effective? Do they provide useful information for course planning? Do they provide data on subjective and objective needs? Can the data be translated into content?

⤐

Curriculum area	*Sample questions*
Content	Are the goals and objectives derived from needs analyses?
	If not, from where were they derived?
	Are they appropriate for the specified groups of learners?
	Do the learners think the content is appropriate?
	Is the content appropriately graded?
	Does it take speech processing constraints into account?
Implementation	
Methodology	Are the materials, methods and activities consonant with the prespecified objectives?
	Do the learners think the materials, methods and activities are appropriate?
Resources	Are resources adequate/appropriate?
Teacher	Are the teacher's classroom management skills adequate?
Learners	Are the learning strategies of the students efficient?
	Do learners attend regularly?
	Do learners pay attention, apply themselves in class?
	Do learners practise their skills outside the classroom?
	Do the learners appear to be enjoying the course?
	Is the timing of the class and the type of learning arrangement suitable for the students?
	Do learners have personal problems which interfere with their learning?
Assessment and evaluation	Are the assessment procedures appropriate to the prespecified objectives?
	Are there opportunities for self-assessment by learners? If so, what?
	Are there opportunities for learners to evaluate aspects of the course such as learning materials, methodology, learning arrangement?
	Are there opportunities for self-evaluation by the teacher?

In considering the 'who' question, a number of candidates emerge. Depending on the size and scope of the evaluation, all or some of these may play a part. In the first instance, outside authorities such as government bodies or funding agencies may play a role. Programme administrators at a local level (such as heads of centres or teachers-in-charge) may be involved. Teachers, and, in learner-centred systems, the learners themselves will certainly be involved. Other participants may include outside experts, observers or interested parties. Teachers may wish occasionally to involve their colleagues in peer observation of lessons, or parts of lessons.

As already indicated, evaluation as a process in its own right, rather than as a final product of the curriculum process, may take place at any time, from the planning stage onward. In a learner-centred curriculum, where much of the curriculum activity will be conducted at a local level, the bulk of the evaluation should take the form of informal monitoring by the teacher with the cooperation of the learners.

The tools and techniques for evaluation will be many and varied. They may include standardised tests of various sorts, along with questionnaires, observation schedules of classroom interaction, interview schedules, learner diaries and so on. The most important thing is that the tool selected should be appropriate to the task. In the final section of this chapter, we shall look at some of the techniques for stimulating self-assessment of their own progress by learners, and also tools for the evaluation by learners of materials, learning activities and learning arrangements. (For an overview of the range of instruments available for various sorts of assessment and evaluation see Brindley 1986.)

8.4   The Assessment of Second-Language Proficiency

We now turn to an area of assessment which is rather controversial. This is the assessment of second-language proficiency. In so doing, we shall raise a number of central issues in language teaching and testing. This section builds on the discussion in 8.2 relating to the construct validation of language tests and also to the discussion of proficiency in 3.5. Acknowledgement is made to Brindley (1986) for his evaluation of the assessment of second-language proficiency.

It was noted in 3.5 that proficiency is essentially about being able to do things with language. This rather programmatic definition becomes problematic when we turn to the issue of proficiency assessment.

In order to assess any area of human behaviour, it is necessary to have some idea of what it is we are trying to assess. What is it that testers of proficiency are trying to assess? We can get some idea by looking at the instruments they have developed. One such instrument is the proficiency rating scale. What follows is the generic description of speaking proficiency at an intermediate-high level. It is taken from the American Council on the Teaching of Foreign Languages Provisional Proficiency Guidelines.

> Able to satisfy most survival needs and limited social demands.
> Shows some spontaneity in language production but fluency is very uneven.
> Can initiate and sustain a general conversation but has little understanding of the social conventions of conversation.
> Developing flexibility in a range of circumstances beyond immediate survival needs.
> Limited vocabulary range necessitates much hesitation and circumlocution.
> The commoner tense forms occur but errors are frequent in formation and selection.
> Can use most question forms.
> While some word order is established, errors still occur in more complex patterns.
> Cannot sustain coherent structures in longer utterances or unfamiliar situations.
> Ability to describe and give precise information is limited.
> Aware of basic cohesive features such as pronouns and verb inflections, but many are unreliable, especially if less immediate in reference.
> Extended discourse is largely a series of short, discrete utterances.
> Articulation is comprehensible to native speakers used to dealing with foreigners, and can combine most phonemes with reasonable comprehensibility, but still has difficulty in producing certain sounds in certain positions or in certain combinations, and speech will usually be laboured.
> Still has to repeat utterances frequently to be understood by the general public.
> Able to produce some narration in either past or future.
>
> (Cited in Savignon and Berns 1984:228–229)

In introducing the Australian Second Language Proficiency Rating Scale (ASLPR), Ingram defines proficiency as the mobilisation of linguistic knowledge to carry out communication tasks. Statements of proficiency must therefore be made in behavioural terms. According to Ingram, the scale is designed to measure a construct he calls 'general proficiency'. Such a construct is defined and defended in the following way:

> . . . language occurs only in situations, and, if the proficiency descriptions are related to particular situations, one could be accused of measuring only proficiency in specific situations i.e. one would not be measuring general proficiency, but proficiency in specific registers. On the other hand, language varies from situation to situation; it varies according to who is using it, to whom and about

what subject . . . in other words, it would seem as though one cannot speak of general proficiency so much as proficiency in a language in this situation or that, in this register or that. Yet such a view would seem to be counter-intuitive. If we say that X speaks Chinese . . . we do not mean that X can only give a lecture on engineering in Chinese . . . Rather, when we say that someone can speak a language, we mean that that person can speak the language in the sorts of situations people commonly encounter. That is, there are certain everyday situations in which we, as human beings living in a physical and social world, are necessarily involved . . . General proficiency, then, refers to the ability to use the language in these everyday, non-specialist situations.

(Ingram 1984:10–11)

Here, then, is an applied linguist who is prepared to be quite explicit about the concept of proficiency. Ingram is postulating the existence of an underlying, unobservable construct called 'general proficiency' which, because it is unobservable, must be inferred from learners' performance in specific situations. However, it is not to be confused with the ability to perform in specified situations (i.e. it is more than an achievement test): 'the ASLPR seeks to measure the underlying general proficiency rather than the fulfilment of an absolutely specified task in an absolutely specified situation' (*ibid.*). Learners must therefore be given the opportunity of performing in situations and contexts with which they are familiar.

What precisely is it that we are assessing in making our rating of a given learner? We know that it is not specific situational or contextual knowledge, so presumably this lets out lexical knowledge and the ability to discuss certain topics or themes. What is left when these are taken away are global, impressionistic judgements of the learner's current stage of development in a number of areas including morphological and syntactic development, fluency, pronunciation, sociocultural knowledge, mastery of discourse and so on. All proficiency scales have this same mixture of factors from diverse domains. Carroll (1981), for instance, lists size, complexity, range, speed, flexibility, accuracy, appropriacy, independence, repetition and hesitation. These are generally all rendered down into a single numerical index or descriptor such as '1+' or 'Novice–Low'. The 'general language ability' underlying proficiency scales look suspiciously like Oller's (1979) unitary competence construct, a construct which is dealt with later.

Ingram defines 'general proficiency' in terms of the ability of the learner to carry out tasks in 'certain everyday situations in which we, as human beings living in a physical and a social world are necessarily involved . . .' General proficiency then, refers to the ability to use the language in these everyday, non-specialist situations. However, it could be argued that this ability does not necessarily represent an ability which all language learners have but is, in fact, simply another register.

Another difficulty with proficiency scales is related to the means whereby learners are assessed. This is generally through some form of oral interview. However, it is difficult to see how such interviews can allow one to make valid judgements about the learner's ability to carry out real-world tasks.

Let us look in greater detail at the sample description taken from the ACTFL scale. According to the scale, the learner, at 'Intermediate–High' level is able to satisfy survival needs and limited social needs. At this level, the learner's performance will be characterised by the following features which are extracted from the list set out on p. 124:

- can satisfy some survival needs and limited social demands
- shows some spontaneity
- fluency is very uneven
- can initiate and sustain a general conversation
- has little understanding of the social conventions of discourse
- has limited vocabulary range
- commoner tense forms occur, but errors are frequent in formation and selection
- can use most question forms
- basic word order is established
- errors occur in more complex patterns
- cannot sustain coherent structures in longer utterances
- has limited ability to describe and give precise information
- is aware of basic cohesive feature
- extended discourse is largely a series of short, discrete utterances
- articulation is comprehensible to native speakers used to dealing with foreigners
- can combine most phonemes with reasonable comprehensibility
- has difficulty in producing certain sounds in certain positions or in certain combinations
- speech will usually be laboured
- has to repeat utterances frequently to be understood by the general public
- can produce some narration in either past or future

The vague, impressionistic speech features are indicators of the postulated 'general proficiency' which is driving the user's communication skills. These features manifest themselves in tasks such as the following:

> - coping with less routine situations in shops, post office, bank (e.g. asking for a larger size, returning an unsatisfactory purchase) and on public transport (e.g. asking passenger where to get off for unfamiliar destination)

  - explaining some personal symptoms to a doctor
  - communicating routine needs and basic details of unpredictable occurrences.

(Ingram 1984:43)

The use of such scales is fraught with hidden dangers. The scales themselves tend to take on ontological status (that is, there is a tendency to assume that such a construct as 'survival proficiency' really exists, rather than being something constructed to account for observable or hypothetical features of learners' speech). The scales themselves have not been empirically validated to determine if learners really do act in the ways described by the scales, nor have the task types been validated. For example, is the task of 'returning an unsatisfactory purchase' of the same order of difficulty as 'explaining some personal symptoms to a doctor' as suggested by the scale? Do the two tasks draw on the same linguistic and communicative resources? How do we test for these things? As already pointed out, most ratings are conducted through an oral interview. While these will provide us with information on the learner's ability to take part in interviews, they are unlikely to tell us much about the learner's ability to 'explain personal symptoms to a doctor', or to 'ask passenger where to get off for unfamiliar destination'.

To summarise, then, proficiency refers to the ability to perform certain communicative tasks with a certain degree of skill. Degree of skill will be determined by mastery of a complex set of enabling skills which will include syntax and morphology, fluency, socio-cultural knowledge, phonology, and discourse. Whether or not these can or should be taught, or whether they will emerge spontaneously as a function of learning to perform certain communicative acts is a hotly-debated issue at the present time.

A popular means of assessing proficiency is the use of rating scales. A subjective and impressionistic assessment of the learner's current 'general proficiency' level is made through an oral interview. Level of proficiency is set by such performance factors as fluency, mastery of syntax and so on. These are assumed to correlate with the ability to perform real-world tasks. However, the link between performance factors and task difficulty has never been empirically validated. In addition, the degree to which skills mastered in one domain transfer to another is open to dispute. We must assume that some transfer occurs (otherwise there would hardly be any point in teaching).

The only performance factors to have been subjected to extensive empirical validation are syntax and morphology. Here, it has been found that proficiency descriptions are at odds with what learners actually do at different stages (Johnston 1985).

It would seem that the construct of general proficiency must draw a large part of its theoretical rationale from an assumption that the construct itself is a single psychological entity, in much the same way as the construct of 'verbal intelligence' is assumed to be a single psychological entity. Without this assumption, it is difficult to see how claims about the comparability of different performance factors and task types could be made.

In fact, unlike proficiency scales, the question of whether or not a single construct underlies the ability to use language has been empirically investigated, and it is to these investigations that we now turn.

The name most commonly associated with research into the factorial structure of language proficiency is John Oller. Oller suggested that a single psychological construct underlay language proficiency. He called this construct a 'pragmatic expectancy grammar', and characterised it in the following manner:

> Language use is viewed as a process of interacting plans and hypotheses concerning the pragmatic mapping of linguistic contexts onto extralinguistic ones. Language learning is viewed as a process of developing such an expectancy system.
>
> (Oller 1979:50)

Oller put his theory to the test by utilising procedures similar to those used in intelligence testing. He analysed the scores of language learners on a wide range of tests to determine the degree of correlation between them (correlation refers to the degree to which subject scores on one test co-vary with scores on another test).

Oller's aim was to test which of three possible hypotheses about language learning were supported by the data. These hypotheses were as follows:

Hypothesis 1: The Divisibility Hypothesis: Language proficiency consists of a number of discrete skills.

Hypothesis 2: The Indivisibility Hypothesis: Proficiency consists of a single skill.

Hypothesis 3: The Partial Divisibility Hypothesis: In addition to a general skill, common to all areas of language use, there will be skills uniquely related to various language modalities.

In order to test these hypotheses, Oller set himself the task of finding:

> ... testing procedures that will generate variances that are unique to tests that are supposed to measure different things. Either the indivisibility hypothesis or the partial divisibility hypothesis allows for a large general factor (or component of variance) common to all language tests. The difference between these alternatives is that the indivisibility hypothesis allows only for a general component of test variance. Once such a component is accounted for, the

> indivisibility hypothesis predicts that no additional reliable variance
> will remain to be accounted for.
>
> (Oller 1979:425)

By subjecting his data to factor analysis, Oller found that, 'once the general factor predicted by the indivisibility (or unitary competence) hypothesis was extracted, essentially no meaningful variance was left in any of the tests' (*op cit.*:429). The indivisibility hypothesis was thus upheld.

In non-statistical terms, the results suggested that performance on tests of, say, reading, draw on the same underlying language skill as tests of listening; or that aspects of a macro-skill (such as pronunciation, fluency, control of syntax and vocabulary for 'speaking') are all part of an underlying 'proficiency'.

The implications of such a finding for language teaching were unequivocal. If all language performance derived from a single underlying psychological construct, then differentiated curricula (including needs-based courses) were redundant, and efforts to develop such courses a waste of time. The only thing needed would be a series of learning tasks which engaged the learner's interest and which were at the appropriate level of difficulty.

Emboldened by his findings, Oller went so far as to suggest that:

> Implications of the foregoing findings for education are sweeping. They suggest a possible need for reform that would challenge some of the most deeply seated notions of what school is about – how schools fail and how they succeed. The potential reforms that might be required if these findings can be substantiated are difficult to predict. Clearly they point us in the direction of curricula in which the focus is on the skills required to negotiate symbols rather than on the 'subject matter' in the traditional sense of the term. They point away from the medieval notion that psychology, grammar, philosophy, English, history and biology are intrinsically different subject matters. Physics and mathematics may not be as reasonably distinct from English literature and sociology as the structure of universities implies.
>
> (Oller 1979:457)

As it turned out, follow-up research has not substantiated Oller's findings. In 1983, Vollmer and Sang were able to demonstrate that, on statistical grounds alone, Oller's results were suspect. Since then, research such as that reported by Bachman and Mack (1986) suggests that proficiency consists of a number of factors which are related to each other in extremely complex ways. At present the consensus seems to be that proficiency is a multidimensional construct. Brindley (1986) suggests that the unitary/divisibility debate: »»→

... has now been substantially resolved in favour of a multidimensional view, allowing, however, for the existence of a weaker general factor than was originally postulated.

(Brindley 1986:11)

8.5   Techniques for Self-Assessment

A major reason for carrying out assessment and evaluation is to determine whether learners are progressing satisfactorily or not, and, if they are not, to diagnose the cause or causes and suggest remedies.

In a learner-centred system, learners can be sensitised to their role as learner, and can also be assisted to develop as autonomous learners by the systematic use of self-assessment. Self-assessment techniques also help learners identify preferred materials and ways of learning. They can be involved in evaluating most aspects of the curriculum, including their own progress, the objectives of the course, the materials and learning activities used, the learning modes and so on, although there is some evidence that the development of self-assessment and self-monitoring may be quite difficult for some learner types such as those with little formal education (Burton and Nunan 1986).

In order for students to assess their own performance, they must know what it is they are being taught. For this reason, if for no other, the objectives of the course should, at some stage, be formulated and made available to the learners in a way they can understand. One value of objectives, formulated in terms of real-world and pedagogic tasks and communicative skills, as described in Chapter 5, is that learners can identify with them more readily than with objectives formulated in linguistic terms. Such objectives would not necessarily be couched in the same terms as they appear in a teacher's programme. They may take the forms shown in Tables 8.3 and 8.4, and may also be translated into the learner's first language.

TABLE 8.3

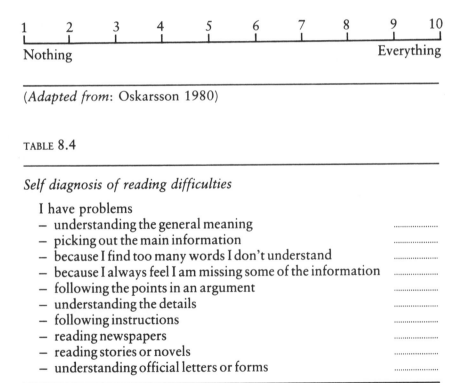

Self-assessment of proficiency

1 I can ask for factual information.	YES	NO
2 I can provide personal details.	YES	NO
3 I can understand weather forecasts on the radio.	YES	NO
4 I can read public notices.	YES	NO

Imagine you are watching a television show in English with subtitles. Suddenly the subtitles disappear.

How much would you understand?

1   2   3   4   5   6   7   8   9   10

Nothing   Everything

(*Adapted from*: Oskarsson 1980)

TABLE 8.4

Self diagnosis of reading difficulties

I have problems
- understanding the general meaning   ....
- picking out the main information   ....
- because I find too many words I don't understand   ....
- because I always feel I am missing some of the information   ....
- following the points in an argument   ....
- understanding the details   ....
- following instructions   ....
- reading newspapers   ....
- reading stories or novels   ....
- understanding official letters or forms   ....

The students' self awareness as learners can also be developed through being encouraged to undertake systematic self-evaluation of activities, materials and learning arrangements. Low-key self-evaluation scales such as those shown in Tables 8.5, 8.6 and 8.7 can be developed and used by classroom teachers for this purpose.

TABLE 8.5

Self-Evaluation of learning activities
Tick the box

Activity	I like	It's OK	I don't like
Listening to authentic conversations			
Watching the TV news			
Singing songs			
Doing grammar			
Doing pronunciation			
Doing drills in the language lab			
Doing group work			
Doing role-plays			
Playing games			
Writing letters			
Reading the newspaper			

TABLE 8.6

Self-Evaluation of materials

Tick the box

Activity	I like	It's OK	I don't like
Worksheets			
Videotapes			
Cassette recordings			
Strategies			
Streamline			
Listen to Australia			
Situational English			

TABLE 8.7

Learning arrangement rating scale

Directions: Rate the following learning arrangements according to the following scale 5 – I like this very much, 4 – I like this a lot, 3 – it's OK, 2 – I don't like this much, 1 – I don't like this at all.

Full-time day classes	1	2	3	4	5
Part-time day classes	1	2	3	4	5
Part-time evening classes	1	2	3	4	5
Learning at home	1	2	3	4	5
Learning by correspondence	1	2	3	4	5
In class, I prefer					
– whole class work	1	2	3	4	5
– small group work	1	2	3	4	5
– pair work	1	2	3	4	5
– learning alone	1	2	3	4	5

In order to foster out-of-class language use, learners should be encouraged to monitor the degree to which they manage to use the target language in the community, and also the types of encounters where they used the language. Learner diaries can be constructed for such purposes. These need not be elaborate, as the Table 8.8 demonstrates.

TABLE 8.8

Learner diary

Directions: Complete one diary sheet each week

This week I studied
This week I learned
This week I used my English in these places
This week I spoke with these people
This week I made these mistakes
My difficulties are
I would like to know
My learning and practising plans for next week are

8.6   Conclusion

In this chapter, we have looked at the place of assessment and evaluation in a curriculum model based on a learner-centred view of language learning. The chapter addresses some key theoretical and conceptual issues relating to evaluation, which is seen as a crucial element within any curriculum process. It is argued that, in any system claiming to be learner-centred, localised evaluation process involving both teachers and learners need to be developed. Learners need to assess their own progress, and also need to be encouraged to evaluate, from their own perspective, other elements within the curriculum including materials, activities and learning arrangements. Such learner-centred evaluation will assist in the development of a critical self-consciousness by learners of their own role as active agents within the learning process. This, as we saw earlier, is, along with the development of language skills, one of the twin goals of the learner-centred curriculum. Suggestions are made in the two final sections of the chapter on how low-key evaluations and assessment by teachers and learners might be carried out.

This chapter is also concerned with examining some of the problems associated with the assessment of language proficiency, an important concern in any teaching programme which conceives of language in performance, or behavioural, terms. While acknowledging the importance of proficiency rating scales for making broad generalisations about where a learner is situated on a scale from non-user to equivalent to native speaker status, criticisms are made of the current state of proficiency assessment. It is suggested that the construct of 'general proficiency' needs clarification, and assessment measures need to be validated against what learners can actually do at any given stage of development. One of the central problems of such scales, if one rejects a view of proficiency as a unitary construct, is that there will be variability amongst learners at any given time. Thus, learners will vary, not only in terms of the tasks they are able to carry out, but also on broader measures, relating to mastery of macro-skills and individual components of proficiency (such as fluency, mastery of syntax and morphology, ability to operationalise sociocultural knowledge, conversational tactics and so on). Obviously, a great deal of further research needs to be done in this area.

9 Evaluation and Professional Development

9.1 Introduction

Within a learner-centred system, the teacher has a central role to play in all aspects of the curriculum. In systems based on traditional curriculum models, the teacher is very often reduced to the role of servant to a centralised curriculum process in which decisions about what will be taught, how it will be taught and how learner assessment and course evaluation will be conducted are made, not by teachers, but by some authority remote from the point of course delivery.

In a learner-centred system, such centralised direction is undesirable. It is also hardly feasible, as a central assumption of the learner-centred philosophy is that differentiated curricula will have to be developed to respond to differentiated learner needs, the differentiation occurring along many different dimensions. Even curricula which share common linguistic content may well be differentiated in terms of topics, themes, situations, methodology, materials, learning tasks and activities, learning arrangements, means of assessment and so on.

In this work, I have attempted to view curriculum processes from a number of different perspectives. Minimally, the curriculum can be seen as a plan of action (the planned curriculum), as a description of what actually happens in classrooms (the implemented curriculum), and as an analysis and description of what learners actually learn (the assessed curriculum). (See also Bartlett and Butler's (1985) comprehensive curriculum model.) The planned curriculum relates to what is set down in curriculum documents and plans; the implemented curriculum is what actually happens during the teaching learning process; and the assessed curriculum is what the learners actually learn. In an ideal world, these three curricula would be identical. In other words, what was planned would be what actually got learned, there would be no unanticipated outcomes, and learners would learn everything they were taught.

To assume that this is the way things work in reality is hopelessly naive. One thing we do know about the curriculum at present is that teaching does not equal learning. However, this does not mean that we should not strive to bring the planned, the implemented and the assessed curriculum into alignment. In this chapter we shall look at some of the ways in which we might work towards this ideal.

In the three sections which make up the bulk of this chapter, we shall look at evaluation processes in relation to the three aspects of the curriculum process already described. In doing so, a view of 'teacher as curriculum developer' will be articulated. It will be argued that a central weakness in most curriculum models is the lack of articulation between (or, in some cases, even recognition of) the planned, implemented and assessed curriculum. Lack of articulation means that the possibility of the implemented and assessed curricula affecting the planned curriculum is severely constrained.

In addition to being key curriculum development agents in a learner-centred system, classroom teachers are uniquely placed to integrate the implemented and assessed curricula with the planned curriculum. However, they will be in a position to do this only if they have appropriate skills and techniques for documenting and analysing what is happening in the classroom during the learning process, and for assessing learner progress.

In the final section of the chapter, we shall look at the professional development aspects of the teacher as curriculum developer.

9.2 Evaluation and the Planning Process

One of the themes of this book is the need to see all of the elements within the curriculum process as interrelated. A major weakness of the 'ballistic' curriculum model, described in Chapter 2, is that each element within the model is sequential. Succeeding elements are therefore incapable of influencing the ones which precede them.

In the model proposed here, while certain activities logically precede others, there is much greater integration. In particular, the monitoring and evaluation element needs to be seen as parallel with all other elements rather than occurring simply as an appendage to the instructional process.

The planning process involves initial data collection from which are derived goals, objectives and learning content. These processes and their attendant techniques were described in Chapters 4 and 5.

As we saw in the previous chapter (Section 8.3), the principal purpose for evaluating the planned curriculum is to determine the efficacy of the planning procedures employed, and also to assess whether the content and objectives are appropriate. While such questions can be comprehensively answered only in relation to the implemented curriculum, some evaluative work can be carried out before a course begins.

At a relatively informal level, survey forms can be circulated to colleagues who have had experience in course planning at different levels. If counsellors are available, they should also be consulted. At a slightly more formal level, if detailed instruments and questionnaires have been developed, they should be trialled with a range of learners before being introduced.

Content, including objective grids, can be compared with the specifications set out for other programmes aimed at similar learner groups. Grading appropriacy can also be checked against other syllabus outlines and published coursebooks.

9.3   Evaluation and the Implemented Curriculum

Whereas the planned curriculum is located in the curriculum documents and statements of intent of curriculum developers, the implemented curriculum is found in the classroom itself, where it is manifested in the content, resources and processes of learning. It has been suggested that in an ideal world the planned curriculum will be faithfully reflected in the teaching–learning situation, but that in the real world, the planned curriculum will be transformed by such things as the hidden agendas of the learners, the moment-by-moment realities of the learning process and the decisions made by teachers on the spur of the moment as they monitor and react to unfolding classroom events.

It is crucially important to study the classroom and the interactions which occur within it because for the majority of learners, and also for many teachers, the classroom represents reality. For them, the implemented curriculum *is* the curriculum, and the planned curriculum is often either invisible or unreal.

We need to study the implemented curriculum for a number of reasons. The most important of these is that it is the implemented, rather than the planned curriculum, which will determine the assessed curriculum. That is, the learners' classroom experiences will be more important than statements of intent in determining learning outcomes.

Some of the most interesting classroom investigations currently being undertaken are those by second language acquisition researchers whose work was referred to in Chapter 5. One such researcher has this to say about such research:

> While still in its youth, if not infancy, classroom-centred research has already accumulated a substantial body of knowledge about what actually goes on in ESL classrooms, as opposed to what is believed to go on, and as distinct from what writers on TESL methods tell us ought to go on.
>
> (Long 1983:422)

The point Long is making is that the direct study of classroom processes reveals data that can not be obtained in any other way. It has been found that not only is there a disparity between the planned curriculum (what the curriculum planners suggest should go on) and the implemented

,curriculum (what actually does go on), but there are also disparities between what teachers believe happens in class and what actually happens. For example, Nunan (1986c) studied a number of 'communicative' classrooms and found that, in fact, there was very little happening in these classes which could be called 'communicative' language use.

This point can be illustrated by looking at two examples from the data which were collected.

One of the characteristics of genuine communication is the use of referential questions (questions to which the questioner does not know the answer). In the Nunan data, a study of the lesson plans (the planned curriculum) indicated that the lessons under study were 'communicative' in the sense that this term is used in Chapter 3. Thus the first lesson was based on an 'information-gap' activity in which learners had to share information to complete a problem. The second lesson centred on a study of a street map. However, when the patterns of interaction, particularly in the teacher-fronted parts of the lessons are examined, it is seen that they are basically non-communicative. The teacher nominates the topics as well as who is to speak, and the questions are almost exclusively of the display type (questions to which the questioner already knows the answer).

Here is the teacher in Lesson 1 introducing the class to the information-gap activity.

> T: today, er, we're going to um, we're going to do something where, we, er, listen to a conversation and we also talk about the subject of the conversation er, in fact, we're not going to listen to one conversation, how many conversations are we going to listen to?
> S: three
> T: how do you know?
> S: because, er, you will need, er, three tapes and three points
> T: three?
> S: points
> T: what?
> S: power points
> T: power points, if I need three power points and three tape recorders, you correctly assume that I'm going to give you three conversations, and that's true, and all the conversation will be different, but they will all be on the same . . .?
> Ss: subject, subject
> T: the same . . . ?
> S: subject, subject
> T: right, they will all be on the same subject

(Nunan 1986c:5–6)

It can be seen that the teacher knows (or thinks he knows) the appropriate answer to all the questions asked. In terms of the interaction patterns, this extract is typical of the whole lesson. The teacher is firmly in control of who says what when. This is not a criticism. The teacher in question is highly experienced, and is a particularly skilled classroom performer. His elicitation (or corkscrew) technique, which makes the students do a great deal of the work, is admirable. The point is, however, that the exchanges are essentially non-communicative, despite the best intention of the teacher.

The next extract is taken from a lesson on map reading. The class is at a much lower level than the other, and the teacher is somewhat less experienced. However, the patterns of interaction are very similar. In the following extract, we see a rather less successful attempt at elicitation than in the first.

> T: ok, where is John Martin's? Phung? John Martin's?
> S: oh, Gawler Pla(ce)
> Ss: Gawler Place
> T: John Martin's?
> S: Gawler Place
> T: Gawler Place? no!
> S: (inaudible)
> T: Charles . . .?
> S: Charles
> T: Street
> S: Charles Street and, er, Rundle Mall
> T: Rundle Mall, yeah, so it's on the ... ?
> S: on the, on the corner of, on the corner
> T: on the corner of ... ? Charles Street
> S: Charles Street
> T: and?
> S: and
> T: Rundle Mall, yeah, yeah? John Martin's is on the corner of Charles Street and Rundle Mall

Here, the teacher not only does most of the work, he ends up answering his own original question.

Classroom data such as these demonstrate that there is a gap between the rhetoric of the planned curriculum and the reality of the classroom, and that teachers are very often unaware of this gap. While it could be claimed that they are rather isolated examples from which it is dangerous to generalise, they do, in fact, accord with several similar studies. Long and Sato, for instance, found that:

> ESL teachers continue to emphasise form over meaning, accuracy
> over communication. This is illustrated, for example, by the
> preference for display over referential questions and results in
> classroom NS-NNS conversation which differs greatly from its
> counterpart outside classrooms.

(Long and Sato 1983:283–284)

(The reader is also referred to Chaudron (1988) and van Lier (1988) for two excellent although quite different treatments of classroom-centred research.)

It has been suggested that the gap between intention and reality is a result of the powerful constraints which exist within the context of the classroom. In discussing the differences that exist between language used inside the classroom and that used outside, Seliger suggests:

> These differences are the necessary result of the organisation of contexts for the formal teaching of language that takes place inside the classroom. Outside the classroom, however, in naturalistic environments, language is a means to an end . . . The language classroom is, by definition, a contrived context for the use of language as a tool of communication. The bulk of time in a language class is devoted to practising language for its own sake because the participants in this activity realise that that is the expressed purpose of their gathering together in a room with a blackboard and a language expert, the teacher.
>
> (Seliger 1983:250–251)

The other major reason for the gap between the planned and implemented curriculum is that very often learners have their own 'hidden agendas' which run counter to the 'official curriculum'. It has been hypothesised that these hidden agendas determine output from the learners' perspective regardless of input (Burton and Nunan 1986).

One way of closing the gap between intention and reality would be to abandon the planned curriculum altogether. However, this is unlikely to lead to more systematic and rational approaches to the curriculum. It would be far better to develop strategies to bring intention and reality into line.

One way of doing this would be to make the planned curriculum very explicit to the learners, using bilingual resources where necessary to get the message across. It could well be that learners develop their own hidden curricula because they have little idea of the nature of the official curriculum. This is the view of Candlin and Edelhoff:

> We assume that learners learn most when they are quite precisely aware of what it is that they have to achieve, and, importantly, how their efforts are to be judged and evaluated. We could add, as a rider, that learners are more likely to meet this condition when they have been party to the setting of their goals . . .
>
> (Candlin and Edelhoff 1982:vi)

In addition, the planned curriculum needs to be 'learnable'. While we are still ignorant of all the constraints on learnability, a body of literature on the subject is beginning to be developed. Thus Johnston (1985) has been able to demonstrate that the planned curriculum often fails, in terms of learners' mastery of syntax and morphology, because the learners are confronted with items which are simply unlearnable at any given stage (see also Pienemann 1985).

9.4 Evaluation and the Assessed Curriculum

In this section we shall look at some practical techniques for assessing student progress. One of the most important and useful ways of assessing achievement in a communicative curriculum is to set performance-based tests which require learners to demonstrate an ability to carry out those tasks which have been specified in the planned curriculum. It is to facilitate the assessment of communicative performance that the use of performance objectives was advocated in Chapter 5. These objectives need not be formulated before the class begins, but can be constructed during the course itself, once ongoing needs analysis has provided a more realistic picture of likely learner achievement levels.

In Chapter 5 it was suggested that performance objectives should contain three elements: task, conditions and standards. The following example was provided:

> In a classroom role play (condition), students will exchange greetings with the teacher (task). Utterances will be comprehensible to someone used to dealing with a second-language speaker (standard).

It is not always feasible, particularly in large classes, to formally test all learners on a performance basis. In such classes it is useful to involve learners in assessment by teaching them the sorts of self-assessment techniques described in the preceding section.

Observation techniques are also useful in assisting teachers to monitor student progress. However, observation needs to be systematic. This can be facilitated through the use of various forms of rating scales and checklists, samples of which are shown in Table 9.1. These can be kept for each learner in the class, and can be completed at regular intervals during the course.

TABLE 9.1

Sample rating scales

Indicate the degree to which learners contribute to small-group discussions or conversation classes by circling the appropriate number.

(Key: 5 – outstanding, 4 – above average, 3 – average, 2 – below average, 1 – unsatisfactory)

1	The learner participates in discussions.	1	2	3	4	5
2	The learner uses appropriate non-verbal signals.	1	2	3	4	5
3	The learner's contributions are relevant.	1	2	3	4	5
4	The learner is able to negotiate meaning.	1	2	3	4	5
5	The learner is able to convey factual information.	1	2	3	4	5
6	The learner can give personal opinions.	1	2	3	4	5
7	The learner can invite contributions from others.	1	2	3	4	5
8	The learner can agree/disagree appropriately.	1	2	3	4	5
9	The learner can change the topic appropriately.	1	2	3	4	5

Rate the learner's speaking ability by circling the appropriate number.

1   2   3   4   5   6   7   8   9   10

Incapable of   Carries out simple
carrying out   conversation giving
simple conversation   personal information

Rate the learner's listening ability by circling the appropriate number.

1   2   3   4   5   6   7   8   9   10

Incapable of   Follows simple
following simple   instructions in
instructions   classroom setting

Checklist of reading skills

YES	NO	Recognises Roman script upper/lower case
YES	NO	Identifies numbers in various formats
YES	NO	Comprehends key content words/phrases in context
YES	NO	Retrieves simple factual information from short texts
YES	NO	Comprehends regular sound/symbol relationships
YES	NO	Sight reads key function words
YES	NO	Identifies genre of common texts
YES	NO	Identifies topic of simple text on familiar subject
YES	NO	Uses alphabetical indexes
YES	NO	Follows written instructions

In addition to the sorts of procedures described above, there are many different discrete-point tests available for assessing and diagnosing learning problems in phonology, vocabulary, language structures, discourse and so on. Examples of such tests may be found in the numerous books on language testing.

9.5   Causes of Learner Failure

In this section, we shall take a brief look at a small-scale study designed to investigate teacher attitudes toward the failure of learners to achieve programme goals and objectives.

Background

Assessing learner achievement (or lack thereof) is only the first step in the evaluation process. It is highly unlikely that all learners will make satisfactory progress all of the time (if they do, it is likely that the course is too easy for the group). In cases of failure to achieve objectives, the next step is to diagnose the likely cause or causes, and to suggest remedies.

There are many different possible causes of learner failure. Some of the more common of these, which have been anecdotally reported by teachers, are as follows:

- inefficient learning strategies
- poor attention in class
- irregular attendance
- particular macro-skill problems
- difficulty with discrete language points
- failure to use the language outside class
- faulty teaching techniques
- objectives inappropriate for learners
- materials / learning activities inappropriate for learners
- inappropriate learning arrangement
- personal (non-language) problems of learners (including physical disability.

The Study

In order to obtain more detailed information, the questionnaire shown in Table 9.2 was circulated to a group of teachers taking part in an in-service curriculum workshop. Although assessment was not one of the workshop topics, some discussion of assessment and evaluation did take place prior to the administration of the questionnaire.

TABLE 9.2 SURVEY QUESTIONNAIRE ON CAUSES OF LEARNER FAILURE

Below are listed some possible causes of learner failure. Which of these, in your opinion, are significant factors in the failure of learners to achieve course objectives? Circle the appropriate numbers.

1   Inefficient learning strategies
2   Failure to use the language out of class
3   Irregular attendance
4   Particular macroskill problems
5   Inappropriate learning activities
6   Inappropriate objectives
7   Faulty teaching
8   Poor attention in class
9   Personal (non-language) problems
10 Learner attitude

Results

The results of the survey are set out in Table 9.3. Causes attributable to the teacher are set out separately from those attributable to the learner.

TABLE 9.3 SURVEY RESULTS OF CAUSES OF LEARNER FAILURE (n = 34)

Cause	Number of teachers rating this as a cause of failure	%
Causes attributable to the learner		
Inefficient learning strategies	26	77
Failure to use the language out of class	26	77
Irregular attendance	15	45
Particular macroskill problems	11	32
Poor attention in class	3	9
Personal (non-language) problems	3	9
Learner attitude	1	4
Causes attributable to the teacher		
Inappropriate learning activities	11	32
Inappropriate objectives	9	27
Faulty teaching	8	23

Discussion

From the data it can be seen that, in general, the teachers surveyed placed responsibility for failure firmly with the learners. However, it is worth noting that, in relation to causes attributable to the teacher, one third of those surveyed identified inappropriate learning activities as a possible cause, and approximately a quarter identified inappropriate objectives and faulty teaching as having a significant effect on learning outcomes.

Systematic observation is one way in which teachers can diagnose which of the above reasons are implicated in learner failure. Non-observable problems, such as failure to use language outside class, can be diagnosed through learner diaries and reports (see the preceding chapter for a sample diary).

Interviewing learners from time to time can also help build up a picture of the learner's preferences, strengths and weaknesses (although some students may not always be forthcoming with their class teachers, and it may be more useful to have a counsellor or bilingual assistant conduct interviews). Such interviews can canvass the following issues:

Do you enjoy coming to class?
Which lessons / parts of lessons have been most useful?
What have you enjoyed most?
What things have you learned so far?
What helped you learn?
How do you learn best?
Have your ideas about how you learn changed? How?
Do you enjoy having different teachers?
Which classes give you the things you asked for at the beginning of the course?
Which lesson / parts of lessons are not useful for you?
Do you come to class as often as you can?
Why have you missed some classes?

Having diagnosed problems, the teacher can develop strategies to overcome them. These need not always entail changing the learner. It may well be that objectives, methods, materials and learning arrangements should be changed to accommodate learners. There are of course some causes, such as personal problems learners are having outside class, which teachers may be incapable of changing.

Determining whether or not one's own shortcomings are responsible for learner failure is a sensitive issue as it may well necessitate the involvement of one's peers in observation and discussion. This is a matter of professional development and is taken up in the next section.

9.6 Evaluation and Teacher Development

In this section, we take up a key issue implicit in most of this book. This is the encouragement of self-analysis and evaluation by teachers of their own classroom work as a means of professional self-development. As Stenhouse (1975) suggests, it is not enough that teachers work be studied, they need to study it themselves. Such self-evaluation, when tied to classroom action research, can also make valuable contributions to curriculum development.

Techniques and procedures for self-development include team teaching, recording (audio or video) and analysing segments of classroom interaction, analysis of classes by outside observers and action research.

Many teachers feel threatened by the idea of an outsider observing their classroom performance. This is unfortunate, as it is one of the most useful means of obtaining information about what is working and what is not. The ideal is for two teachers who have mutual trust to observe and report on each other's classes. (In this context, it is worth noting that in the major study reported in Chapter 10, many teachers nominated team teaching as the most valuable means of professional self-development, and yet relatively few had ever actually taken part in a team-teaching exercise.)

It is important for classroom observation to be systematic. This can be facilitated by checklists such as that shown in Table 9.4.

TABLE 9.4 CLASSROOM OBSERVATION CHECKLIST

Directions: During, or after the class you have observed or taken part in, rate the following statements according to how accurately they reflect what went on.

Key: 1 – Does not at all reflect what went on
     2 – Only marginally reflects what went on
     3 – Neutral
     4 – Describes rather well what went on
     5 – Is a totally accurate reflection of what went on

1	There were no cultural misunderstandings.	1	2	3	4	5
2	The class understood what was wanted at all times.	1	2	3	4	5
3	All instructions were clear.	1	2	3	4	5
4	Every student was involved at some point.	1	2	3	4	5
5	All students were interested in the lesson.	1	2	3	4	5
6	The teacher carried out comprehension checks.	1	2	3	4	5
7	Materials and learning activities were appropriate.	1	2	3	4	5
8	Student groupings and sub-groupings were appropriate.	1	2	3	4	5

➤➤➤

9	Class atmosphere was positive.	1	2	3	4	5
10	The pacing of the lesson was appropriate.	1	2	3	4	5
11	There was enough variety in the lesson.	1	2	3	4	5
12	The teacher did not talk too much.	1	2	3	4	5
13	Error correction and feedback was appropriate.	1	2	3	4	5
14	There was genuine communication.	1	2	3	4	5
15	There was teacher skill in organising group work.	1	2	3	4	5
16	There was opportunity for controlled practice.	1	2	3	4	5
17	Students were enthusiastic.	1	2	3	4	5
18	General classroom management was good.	1	2	3	4	5

(*Adapted from an RSA checklist*)

Interest is growing in the use of action research as a tool for teacher and curriculum development. A practical set of procedures for carrying out such research is presented by Kemmis and McTaggart. Their concept of action research is captured in the following statement:

> The linking of the terms 'action' and 'research' highlights the essential feature of the method: trying out ideas in practice as a means of improvement and as a means of increasing knowledge about the curriculum, teaching and learning. The result is improvement in what happens in the classroom and school, and better articulation and justification of the educational rationale for what goes on. Action research provides a way of working which links theory and practice into the one whole: ideas-in-action.
>
> (Kemmis and McTaggart 1982:5)

They suggest that there are four essential steps in carrying out a piece of research, and we can see from these steps that they represent, in microcosm, the different phases of the curriculum development process.

Step 1: Develop a plan of action to improve what is already happening.
Step 2: Act to implement the plan.
Step 3: Observe and document the effects of action in the contexts in which it occurs.
Step 4: Reflect on (evaluate) these effects as a basis for further planning, subsequent action and so on through a succession of cycles.

There are a number of comments worth making about this action-research cycle. In the first place, it is a constructive, evolutionary process, rather than a revolutionary one. It seeks to build on what is already happening rather than tearing down the old and replacing it with the new. Improvement is also seen as a continuous, rather than as a 'one-off' process. Finally, it places responsibility for improvement in the hands of those who control the implemented curriculum, the classroom teachers.

While action research could be conducted privately, with only the teacher being aware of the experiment in progress, Kemmis and McTaggart stress the need for communication between the teacher, other colleagues and the students concerned. (In fact, they advocate the development of joint projects between teachers working on 'problems of mutual concern and consequence'.) They suggest that dialogue is essential for the following reasons:

> It encourages the development of the rationale for the practice under investigation, and for others related to it.
> It helps to allow the enquiry to be seen as a 'project' rather than as a personal and introspective process.
> It helps to clarify unforeseen consequences and ramifications of the work.
> It makes defining the issues easier because explaining the project to others demands clarifying one's own thinking.
> It helps to get moral support and to see the limits of support (others may not be so captivated by the project as oneself).
> It allows others to help and become involved in a constructive participatory way.
> It aids reflection by providing a variety of perspectives on the effects of action and the constraints experienced.
>
> (*op cit.*:13)

Action-research projects can vary enormously in size and scope, as is demonstrated by the following examples. It goes without saying that issues about which one can do nothing should be avoided.

Starting points for action research projects could be as follows:

I have heard that increasing the use of referential rather than display questions stimulates students to use more complex language. Will this work with my students?

I seem to spend too much time talking in class. Can I set up a project to stimulate and monitor student talk?

I would like to sub-divide my class into smaller groups which are more responsive to learner needs. Will this improve the quality of learning?

My learners do not seem to use English outside the class. How can I encourage and monitor language use outside?

Four other teachers at my centre have students at roughly the same proficiency level. Could we pool our resources to develop a more responsive curriculum for these learners?

As a monolingual teacher with a heterogeneous class, can I make use of bilingual strategies and resources? Will these improve learning outcomes?

There is some controversy about whether or not informing students of course objectives improves learning. Can I experiment with my students to determine the affective and cognitive outcomes of providing course objectives?

From these examples, it can be seen that action-research projects can vary enormously in size, complexity and the number of individuals involved in them.

9.7 Conclusion

In this chapter we have looked at the role of the teacher in evaluation. It has been suggested that in a learner-centred system, the teacher has a crucial role to play in both student assessment and course evaluation. It is suggested that evaluation should encompass student outcomes, causes of learning difficulties and possible remediation. Sample techniques for student assessment are presented.

The chapter also advocates teacher self-evaluation, and the use of action research as valuable means of stimulating both teacher and curriculum development.

In the next, and final, chapter we shall take a look at the role of the teacher as curriculum developer. The chapter reports on a national study of teachers as curriculum developers, and shows what teachers think of themselves in such a role.

10 *The Teacher as Curriculum Developer*

10.1 Introduction

The central theme of this book has been that, in a learner-centred educational system, it is the teacher who is the principal agent of curriculum development. In this final chapter we shall look at how teachers respond when cast in this role.

Data for this chapter were derived from a national study of teachers as curriculum developers within the Australian Adult Migrant Education Program. Within the AMEP, a centralised curriculum model had given way to a learner-centred one. The initial question prompting the study was as follows:

What happens when a national language programme abandons its centralised curriculum for a localised learner-centred model?

It quickly became apparent that the most tangible result of the abandonment of a centralised curriculum was fragmentation and perceived lack of continuity in the curriculum. The national study was established to investigate and take steps to remedy perceived shortcomings in the curriculum area. The study thus came to focus on the following questions:

What are the causes of curriculum discontinuity?

What can be done to alleviate these?

Who should be involved in the process of remedying perceived shortcomings in the curriculum?

10.2 The Teacher as Curriculum Developer – A National Study

Background

The study was based on the Australian Adult Migrant Education Program which is one of the largest single-language programmes in the world with annual enrolments in excess of 120,000. In 1980 the AMEP abandoned its centralised curriculum in favour of a localised model which, it was hoped, would facilitate the development of more appropriate courses for the Program's extremely diverse client group. This change in policy required the teacher to become the principal agent of curriculum development.

Within the Program, learners typically attend a given learning arrangement for a 10- or 13-week term, and then either leave the Program or apply for another course. Depending on the state where Program delivery occurs, learners may either be accepted for a second course immediately, or may have to wait for up to a year for another course. There is a great diversity of learning arrangements including full-time, part-time, community classes, courses in industry, self-access courses, a home tutor scheme and individualised learning arrangements.

The idealised curriculum process is for learners to be grouped according to some common criterion or 'need', and for teachers to negotiate content, materials and methodology with the learners. Each course is therefore potentially unique.

In an initial survey, a group of teachers within the Program were asked to nominate who should be primarily responsible for various curriculum processes. The processes investigated were initial needs analysis, goal and objective setting, selecting and grading content, ongoing needs analysis, grouping learners, devising learning activities, instructing learners, monitoring and assessing progress and course evaluation. All of the teachers surveyed felt that they should be the ones primarily responsible for selecting and grading content, devising learning activities and instruction. They also felt that they should be the ones primarily responsible for initial and ongoing needs analysis, goal and objective setting, monitoring and assessment and course evaluation. The only task to which teachers did not accord the highest ranking was that of grouping learners. (The complete set of data from this study are presented in Chapter 3.)

This study indicates quite clearly that the teachers surveyed see themselves as the principal agents of curriculum development. In order to gain greater insights into the problems teachers were encountering in this expanded professional role, and to document the solutions which they see as appropriate, the study detailed in the rest of this chapter was carried out.

Research Methodology

Because the study was looking for insights into the effect of a curriculum policy change on teachers (rather than learners), there was no attempt at the quantification of learning outcomes. Following Beretta, it was felt that the methodology had to be consonant with the fact that evaluation is applied enquiry. Beretta suggests that, given the applied nature of such enquiry:

(a) . . . we conduct our research in the field rather than in artificially controlled 'laboratory' settings, (b) we consider the effect of total programmes rather than isolated components of them, (c) the duration of the studies should be long-term rather than short-term and (d) randomisation is not always practicable or crucial.

(Beretta 1986a:145)

It should also be added that research methods need to be acceptable to and valid for those involved in programme planning, implementation and evaluation (in this case, the classroom practitioner).

Parlett and Hamilton, two of the pioneers of naturalistic, field-based methods in educational evaluation, suggest that a diversity of techniques is needed within this particular paradigm:

Illuminative evaluation is not a standard methodological package, but a general research strategy. It aims to be both adaptable and eclectic. The choice of research tactics follows not from research doctrine, but from decisions in each case as to the best available techniques: the problem defines the methods used, not vice versa. Equally, no method (with its own built-in limitations) is used exclusively or in isolation; different techniques are combined to throw light on a common problem. Besides viewing the problem from a number of angles, this 'triangulation' approach also facilitates the cross-checking of otherwise tentative findings.

(Parlett and Hamilton 1983:16–17)

A final factor influencing the choice of methods was the desirability of involving as many of the 1,500 practitioners involved in the Program as possible.

In the event, the following techniques were used:

- extended interviews and discussions with groups of teachers, administrators and curriculum support personnel working at all levels and in all areas of the programme
- individual interviews with selected personnel
- the administration of a questionnaire to all those involved in professional aspects of programme delivery
- a detailed illuminative case study of one learning arrangement.

In all, just on 300 teachers, administrators and curriculum-support personnel took part in the interviews and discussions, while 568 questionnaires were completed and returned (although not all respondents completed all sections of the questionnaire).

Interviews

The data collection procedure adopted in the interviews and discussions was as follows: sessions were recorded (either on tape or in detailed notes); these were transcribed, and summaries were made of the transcriptions; summaries were returned to those who had been interviewed for verification and amendment before being made public.

A great deal of data was yielded by the interviews. The major points which emerged are reported here.

Although for the six years preceding teachers were supposed to have been the prime agents of curriculum development, there was a great deal of confusion about what was meant by the term curriculum. For many teachers, the term meant a prescriptive body of content. This tendency to view curriculum as content rather than process meant that anyone from a centralised agency turning up in a language centre purporting to deal with 'curriculum' issues was often treated with a great deal of suspicion.

It was evident that curriculum continuity had suffered as a result of the adoption of a localised curriculum model, and that this lack of continuity existed between, as well as within, classes. (Teachers tended to see the lack of continuity as existing between courses, whereas programme administrators tended to see it as a problem within courses.)

Not all teachers saw the lack of continuity as a problem. One teacher suggested that:

> Perhaps lack of continuity between courses at a given level is not a problem. If the student finishes one course and goes on to another at the same level, perhaps it is an advantage for them to be discontinuous.

Most of those interviewed, however, saw lack of continuity for learners as a major problem.

A recurring theme was the lack of a general framework for teachers to conceptualise and integrate what they were doing. 'Eclecticism' seems to have been elevated to the status of an educational movement, as is illustrated in the following quote:

> We have got eclecticism of learners in the class, eclecticism of methodology and eclecticism of learning ... so when I am faced with planning my course, I am faced with these bits and pieces.

Some senior administrators saw the lack of accountability as a major reason for lack of continuity. It was pointed out that the AMEP must be one of the few large-scale educational institutions where there is no control at either end of the learning process (i.e. there is neither a curriculum, nor an examination system).

While some teachers blamed the lack of a centralised curriculum for the lack of continuity, most accepted the fact that a set curriculum could not hope to cater for the extremely diverse client group within the Program. Most also accepted in principle the desirability and advantages of having a negotiated curriculum when dealing with adults.

The importance of consultations with colleagues was a recurring theme during the consultations. When asked what they would do if faced with a group of students with whom they had had little experience (such as an unfamiliar proficiency level), teachers generally reported that they would consult a more experienced colleague. The desirability of team teaching was also articulated by many teachers, although, in fact, comparatively few teachers had ever taught as part of a team or spent any length of time in another teacher's classroom.

There was a great deal of sympathy at all levels for the plight of the inexperienced teacher in a system which demanded that the teachers themselves be curriculum developers. It was felt that they needed more than philosophical statements to guide them. In fact there was some difficulty defining the 'inexperienced' teacher. With changing client groups, most teachers can find themselves to be 'inexperienced' at times.

Another disadvantaged group were the casual teachers who had no security of employment, who were usually required to take a class at short notice, who had no consultation time and who had very little opportunity for systematic professional development.

Teachers also felt that in a learner-centred system they needed supporting resources in areas such as counselling, assessment and referral and curriculum advice.

A widely-articulated view was that effective curriculum development would occur only as a result of effective teacher development. Curriculum personnel, in particular, felt that guidelines, and procedures for local curriculum development, would be effective only if teachers were appropriately trained in their use. One curriculum support unit suggested that the key to professional development was to get teachers to think about and articulate what they are doing.

An issue which emerged repeatedly was the need for more time for teachers to engage in curriculum planning. While there had been a change in philosophy which required teachers to become curriculum developers, there was no concomitant increase in the time available for teachers to engage in course planning, to confer with each other and to survey and counsel students.

Many of the problems encountered, and much of the curriculum discontinuity, were not in fact principally problems of curriculum or pedagogy. They were largely problems of administration, management, counselling and so on. Failure on the part of programme planners and administrators to see all these elements as inextricably intertwined makes rational problem solving impossible.

Questionnaire

The questionnaire, shown in Tables 10.1 and 10.2, was divided into three parts. Part A asked teachers to nominate what they saw as the appropriate participatory structure for a proposed National Curriculum Project to produce curriculum guidelines for the programme. Part B sought opinion on the types of guidelines and other types of curriculum support which might be developed, and Part C asked teachers to provide input on their perceptions of problems and possible solutions to curriculum planning and development.

TABLE 10.1   QUESTIONNAIRE – PART A

Who should carry out the work of the proposed Curriculum Project?

Key: 1 – strongly disagree
     2 – moderately disagree
     3 – neutral
     4 – moderately agree
     5 – strongly agree

1	A small team of persons with curriculum expertise	1	2	3	4	5
2	Teachers with relevant skills	1	2	3	4	5
3	Steering groups of teachers to oversee projects	1	2	3	4	5
4	A mixture of 1, 2 and 3	1	2	3	4	5

The overwhelming consensus from all those responding to this part of the questionnaire was that a mixture of options, including small teams with particular expertise, the secondment of teachers with relevant skills and the utilisation of steering groups made up of teacher representatives, should oversee any projects or tasks which are set up. While it has always been anticipated that any Project outcomes will only succeed if they are derived from instances of successful practice, substantial direct teacher involvement will be possible only if state and territory Adult Migrant Education Services are prepared to pay release time for teachers to carry out tasks and to serve on working parties.

TABLE 10.2 QUESTIONNAIRE – PART B

Rate the following outcomes and tasks on a five point scale from 1 (strongly disagree) through to 5 (strongly agree).

1 The development of curriculum guidelines for inexperienced teachers to follow in developing their courses (the guidelines to be structured around the macroskills of listening, oral interaction, and literacy skills)
2 The development of guidelines for teaching learning strategies and 'learning how to learn'
3 The development of alternative methods for organising teaching and learning (for example, team teaching, peer tutoring, working with mixed ability groups)
4 The identification and documentation of instances of successful curriculum practice from within the Program
5 The development of procedures and instruments for carrying out curriculum tasks (for example, selecting and grading content, selecting learning activities, assessment and evaluation)
6 The development and trialling of a Certificate of ESL for learners
7 The development and trialling of ways of introducing curriculum support personnel including counsellors, bilingual assistants and curriculum advisors
8 The development of curriculum models for different learner groups (for example, new arrivals, intermediate learners)
9 The development of guidelines for different types of program delivery (for example, community classes, English in the workplace, self-access learning)
10 The development and trialling of different procedures for 'micro-planning' (for example, lesson-planning, modular approaches to program design)

Respondents were divided into one of the four following groups, according to their function within the programme:

Group A: teachers whose principal function is programme administration
Group B: teachers whose principal function is curriculum, teacher or materials support
Group C: full-time teachers
Group D: part-time teachers.

The results of the study are set out in Figure 10.1 and Table 10.3. (These results are based on responses received from 458 individuals. These included 39 programme administrators, 19 curriculum support persons, 187 full-time teachers and 213 part-time teachers.)

FIGURE 10.1   RESULTS TO QUESTIONNAIRE – PART B

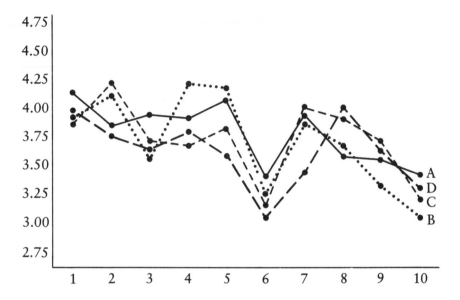

TABLE 10.3   OVERALL RANKINGS OF ITEMS FROM QUESTIONNAIRE – PART B (FROM MOST TO LEAST DESIRABLE).

1   Learning strategy guidelines (Item 2)
2   Guidelines for teaching macroskills (Item 1)
3   Curriculum models for different learner groups (Item 8)
4   Documentation of instances of successful curriculum practice (Item 4)
5   Ways of introducing curriculum support personnel (Item 7)
6   Procedures and instruments for carrying out curriculum tasks (Item 5)
7   Alternative methods for organising teaching/learning (Item 3)
8   Guidelines for different types of program delivery (Item 9)
9   Procedures for 'micro-planning' (Item 10)
10 A Certificate of ESL (Item 6)

There are some interesting differences between the different groups. Both programme administrators and part-time teachers gave a high priority to the development of macro-skill guidelines for inexperienced teachers.

Both groups of teachers, as well as curriculum support personnel, gave a high priority to the development of guidelines for teaching learning strategies and 'learning how to learn', which supports the general view taken in this book that language programmes should have learning goals as well as language goals. All except the curriculum support group gave their lowest rating to the need for a Certificate of ESL, indicating that formalised assessment procedures are seen as less desirable in establishing curriculum continuity than other measures.

From the data presented in the tables, a number of significant points emerge. The first is that there was little real opposition to any of the items listed with the possible exception of Item 10, relating to the development and trialling of an Australian Certificate of ESL. This may have been partly due to the poor wording of the item, which did not clearly indicate that the certificate was intended for learners not teachers.

In general, Item 2, relating to the development of learning strategies and 'learning how to learn' was the most popular item, followed by Item 1 relating to the development of macro-skill guidelines for inexperienced teachers. Once again, due to the construction of the item, it is not immediately apparent whether teachers were responding to the 'guidelines' or the 'inexperienced teacher' part of the item, or both. Another item which gained a high rating was Item 8 relating to different learner groups. It may, in fact, be possible to develop a package which integrates all three of these items.

While the questionnaire allowed for input from greater numbers of teachers than would have been possible had data only been collected through interviews, the results themselves need to be treated with caution. Follow-up interviews indicated that teachers generally disliked quantifying their responses to what they see as complex issues. One group, in fact, which had given a low rating to the idea of a certificate, decided, on discussing the matter in a follow-up interview, that a certificate would be a good idea after all.

Free Form Responses

Section C, soliciting free form comments, was added to the questionnaire to allow teachers to give their perceptions on lack of curriculum continuity and on the notion that teachers were having difficulty implementing the curriculum. It was anticipated that the responses would provide insights into what teachers saw as reasons for lack of continuity.

Responses were coded into the categories in Table 10.4, a category being created whenever there was more than one response which could fit that category. (Sample comments from each category are provided in brackets.) The results are shown in Tables 10.5 and 10.6.

➤➤➤

TABLE 10.4 COMPILATION OF FREE-FORM REASONS GIVEN FOR LACK OF CURRICULUM CONTINUITY

Lack of continuity in the Program is a result of:

1 the philosophy and nature of the Program
   (At present, the curriculum is simply a needs-based philosophy and is interpreted according to the particular needs of students at a particular time.)
2 lack of funding
   (. . . ad hoc arrangements forced by funding demand problems.)
3 lack of appropriate administrative/management support/ coordination ([We need] administrative support for providing continuity.)
4 problems caused by students (e.g. irregular attendance)
   (The stop-start nature of students' attendance creates difficulty.)
5 lack of information for learners about the Program / specific courses
   (Students want to know / be told what is coming up on course and how it connects with their next course.)
6 lack of skills/experience on the part of teachers (including the need for teacher development)
   (We have not really been trained to identify needs.)
7 lack of time for consultation and communication
   (Lack of communication between teachers/centres is a major cause.)
8 high teacher turnover
   (Massive changes of staff . . . have influenced people to respond as they have.)
9 lack of information for teachers about content of previous courses
   ([There is] little evaluation left behind for other teachers to read and find out what has been covered.)
10 courses are too short
    (AME courses are too short.)
11 lack of information and induction for new teachers
    (When one begins work with AMES it is very difficult to find out where everything 'is at'.)
12 rapid changes in TESOL
    (The massive theoretical moves in TESOL over the last fifteen years have left teachers with disparate ideas and models.)
13 lack of support resources (including counselling and bilingual support)
    (Lack of continuity is the result of lack of resources.)
14 lack of curriculum guidelines/models
    (A curriculum model with proven effective ideas and methodologies

and teacher techniques would benefit teachers starting out and may
also be helpful to experienced teachers.)
15 lack of appropriate assessment procedures, including certification
    (We need assessment and evaluation and graded classes.)
16 lack of appropriate materials, including coursebooks
    (A lack of specific materials available for the Australian
    context . . . leads to sporadic programme.)
17 heterogeneous groups and diverse learner types
    (. . . you get a large percentage of students who re-enrol as well as
    some new students which can lead to repetition and lack of
    continuity.)
18 class sizes are too large
    (Class sizes are too big, especially for low levels.)

TABLE 10.5   TOTAL AND PERCENTAGES FOR REASONS PROVIDED

	Administration and curriculum support	*Teachers*	*Total*	*%*
1	7	37	44	9.15
2	3	8	11	2.29
3	8	21	29	6.03
4	4	25	29	6.03
5	4	8	12	2.49
6	10	29	39	8.11
7	5	32	37	7.69
8	1	10	11	2.29
9	4	28	32	6.65
10	8	18	26	5.41
11	0	4	4	0.83
12	3	16	19	3.95
13	5	19	24	4.99
14	11	89	100	20.79
15	2	14	16	3.32
16	2	15	17	3.53
17	3	26	29	6.03
18	0	2	2	0.42

TABLE 10.6   THE FREQUENCY ORDER OF REASONS FOR LACK OF CONTINUITY

1	lack of curriculum guidelines/models
2	the philosophy and nature of the program
3	lack of skills/experience on the part of teachers
4	lack of time for consultation and communication
5	lack of information about previous courses
6	lack of appropriate administrative support
7	problems caused by students
8	heterogeneous groups and diverse learner types
9	courses are too short
10	lack of support resources
11	rapid changes in TESOL
12	lack of appropriate materials
13	lack of appropriate assessment procedures
14	lack of information for learners
15	lack of funding
16	high teacher turnover
17	lack of information and induction for new teachers
18	class sizes are too large

The free form responses largely support the data from Section B of the questionnaire in that respondents clearly favour curriculum guidelines (100 commented on the need for curriculum guidelines models, while nine explicitly stated that they were against the development of guidelines). However, most of those in favour of guidelines stressed the fact that these should be flexible and optional. It is interesting that, while the desirability of developing learning strategies was highly rated in Section B, the lack of guidelines for the teaching of learning strategies was not seen as a cause of lack of continuity.

Identification of the learner-centred philosophy as a major cause of curriculum discontinuity reinforces what was said in interviews. While some of these comments were critical of the philosophy ('A reaction to the current "fashion" of needs-based curriculums.' 'The lack of "continuity" is the result of half-baked attempts to use the AMEP as a "settlement" programme'), most accepted the philosophy and implied that a certain lack of continuity is simply something that we must live with ('The philosophy of a needs-based, learner-centred approach is accepted, but confusion exists as to its implementation.' 'Courses designed for a particular group of learners may not appear to be progressing systematically because they do not follow a set pattern. Each teacher needs to ensure that the progression is, in fact, there, and the processes of needs-based course design are negotiated with the learners . . .').

From the data, it would seem that teachers are asking for the following:

- non-mandatory curriculum guidelines
- a clearer articulation of the practical implications of AMEP policy
- greater in-service provision for the development of programme-planning skills
- more structured time for consultation and communication
- more documentation of course content
- procedures for deriving more homogeneous class groups
- administrative and management procedures which facilitate the implementation of a leaner-centred philosophy
- curriculum design procedures which take account of factors such as the irregular attendance of students
- the provision of learning arrangements which transcend 10–13 week courses
- more adequate support resources, particularly in the areas of counselling, and bilingual and curriculum support
- assistance in dealing with the rapid changes which have taken place in TESOL in the last few years
- more appropriate teaching/learning materials
- more appropriate assessment procedures
- information for learners about the programme / specific courses
- less movement of teaching staff within the programmes
- increased funding
- information and induction procedures for new teachers
- smaller classes.

Sally – A Case Study

In order to provide a sharper focus on curriculum issues as they relate to the teacher, a case study was conducted which looked in detail at one teacher as she went about planning her course. It was hoped that the case study would complement the major points raised in the interviews which were necessarily rather general. While a single case proves very little, evidence from a single instance, if it were to support what teachers were saying in the interviews, and having been provided within a genuine context, would make the case a good deal stronger. If the teacher's experience failed to substantiate the major points which emerged from the interviews, there might be need to examine these more closely.

In searching for a suitable case to illustrate the sorts of problems and solutions with which teachers have to cope in the curriculum area, I felt it desirable to find a teacher who was working with learners who represented an unfamiliar client group. It was assumed that for a teacher working with a familiar type of learner, curriculum problems would not necessarily be particularly salient. In other words, they would not necessarily be recognised as problems.

Fortuitously, at the time that I was searching for a suitable subject, I was approached by a teacher who expressed the need for assistance because she had just been given a group of learners with whom she felt she lacked experience. Data for the case study were provided in a series of interviews carried out during the course.

The Teacher

In order to preserve confidentiality, the teacher will be referred to as 'Sally'. Sally's qualifications include a BA, a DipEd and a post-graduate Diploma in TESL. She has been teaching for 13 years, seven of which have been devoted to the teaching of ESL and EFL to adults. She has taught in Britain, Asia and Australia.

By all criteria, Sally must be considered one of the most experienced and best-qualified teachers in the Program. Despite this, she lacks confidence in her own ability, particularly when working with unfamiliar groups. She has taught on a range of courses, including courses for advanced-level professionals. Despite this, most of her experience has been with low-level, on-arrival groups. When asked whether she considered herself an experienced teacher, she replied, 'Not an experienced all rounder, experienced with some groups.' She was particularly nervous of the group she had been given, an intermediate group of students, most of whom had had several previous courses.

The Class

In order to illustrate the disparate nature of the group, the following sample learner profiles are provided.

Profile 1 A 49-year-old Polish male with nine years of education who has been in Australia for four years. He has had three AMEP courses and is rated at ASLPR 0+ (speaking), 1- (listening). He has not been rated for reading and writing. Client needs are unspecified.

Profile 2 A 59-year-old Greek woman with 14 years of schooling who has been in Australia for 31 years. She has been enrolled in four previous learning arrangements. Her ASLPR ratings are 1 (speaking), 1+ (listening). She has not been rated for reading and writing. She wants general language skills, especially conversation, and is classed as a stabilised learner.

Profile 3 A 27-year-old Chinese male with ten years of education who has been in Australia for three years. He has had one previous course.

His ASLPR ratings for speaking and listening are 1-. Client needs are general language skills, particularly basic conversation.

Profile 4 A 40-year-old Yugoslavian female with eight years of education who has been in Australia for seven years. She has had one previous course, and turned up in the current course three weeks after it had started. ASLPR ratings are 1 (speaking) and 2 (listening).

Profile 5 A 26-year-old Vietnamese male with no formal education. He has had three previous courses and is rated at ASLPR 1 for speaking and listening. He particularly wants speaking skills, and the teacher notes that his pronunciation is particularly poor.

Profile 6 A 26-year-old Kampuchean male with eight years of education who has been in Australia for three years. He has had 11 previous learning arrangements. ASLPR ratings are 1 (speaking), 1+ (listening), 1 (writing), 1 (reading). He can attend only two days a week.

Profile 7 A 24-year-old Vietnamese male with 12 years of formal education who has been in Australia for four months. He has had one previous learning arrangement, and is currently enrolled in two more. ASLPR ratings for speaking and listening are 1.

Profile 8 A 25-year-old Vietnamese female with three years of formal education who has been in Australia for 15 months. She has been enrolled in 20 learning arrangements (many of them concurrent). Her ASLPR ratings are 2 for all skills except reading which is rated at 1+. This student turned up in week six of the course.

Profile 9 A 36-year-old Vietnamese male with eight years of formal education who has been in Australia for six years. He has had three previous learning arrangements. ASLPR ratings are 1+ for all skills except reading which has not been rated.

Profile 10 A 35-year-old Chilean male with six years of formal education who has been in Australia for ten months. He has been enrolled in six learning arrangements. His ASLPR rating is 0+ for speaking and 1- for listening. He wants to focus on developing his listening skills.

Although the class was characterised as consisting of ongoing, intermediate-level learners, the data reveal that they are, in fact, an extremely disparate group. The variations are evident on all the data parameters: there were a range of nationalities; literacy ranged from ASLPR 0+ to 2; some students were reading quite fluently in English while others were illiterate; some learners were considered to be stabilised while others were fast track; some learners were able to attend every day while others, because they had part-time jobs, could attend only twice a week; length of residence in Australia ranged from a few months to 30 years; ages ranged from 26 to 74.

At the Beginning

During the first week of the course the teacher was extremely demoralised. She had been given the data on her class on Friday and started with them on the following Tuesday. The unfamiliar learner profiles, and disparate nature of the group, were making rational planning impossible. She felt that the variables which caused her the most problems were language proficiency and level of literacy. Age was not considered a problem (the 70-year-old was slow while the 68-year-old was a fast learner). Outlook and attitude, particularly degree of confidence, were considered to be the most important variables.

The greatest single problem was the mixed proficiency level which made it impossible to use the same language to explain things to the whole group.

Another major problem was the number of previous courses that students had undertaken. According to the information provided, one student had had 20 different learning arrangements.

Sally took over from another teacher who had had the class for a week. The other teacher provided anecdotal information and lesson plans. However, during the course of the second week, five new students were fed in to make up the numbers, so the information initially provided was not as useful for planning as it might have been. In terms of planning, Sally reported that she would have liked to have met the students and talked to them and then worked out a plan.

One of the things which concerned Sally was the fact that she found it impossible to employ her usual planning procedure, which was to carry out a needs analysis and then develop performance objectives for the group. When asked at the end of her first week what the major problem was she said:

> I don't know where to go to cater for all the variables. During the first week, I've also had problems with group cohesion which may have been solved by forcing more contact. Yesterday, I saw them sitting there as a group of isolated individuals.

She had limited success with trying to find out what the students wanted from the course, and felt that there was more chance of getting them to articulate what they wanted later in the course. In commenting on initial needs-analysis procedures, she stated that:

> It's useful in a limited way, but it's more useful half-way through
> a course, especially with lower level on-arrival students who may
> have very broad goals to start, but as they become accustomed to
> the teacher and the programme they're able to specify what's
> important and necessary. With higher levels . . . I didn't get much
> out of this lot.

Sally felt that those responsible for assigning students to the class should
have done more thorough needs analysis. In fact, in some cases, the
students had not even been given an ASLPR rating.

By the end of the first week, Sally was experiencing a great deal of
frustration. She felt lost, and, in her own words, like a beginning teacher.
When asked what sort of assistance she would like, she replied that all
she wanted was someone who would tell her what to do and how to
cope with the complexities of the professional situation in which she
found herself. She wanted to please her students and do what was best
for each of them, rather than pitching her teaching to a middle level
which would make the class too easy for some and too difficult for others.

When asked whether it would be useful to have someone at centre
level to act as an advisor on curriculum matters, she replied that it would,
but that such a person would:

> . . . have to be someone with a lot of experience, and a lot of
> tolerance for teachers' foibles. Insisting on one particular approach
> is only going to alienate a lot of teachers.

She felt that such a person would be able to look at the students and
give an independent assessment, suggest materials, and basically, 'tell
me what to do with them'.

It is ironic that, under normal circumstances, Sally is the type of teacher
who would be seriously considered for the role of curriculum advisor,
and yet here she was experiencing a great deal of difficulty with her own
students.

At this early point in the course, students had been generally unable
to articulate their needs in any useful fashion, and the teacher was unsure
of whether she should begin by revising what she assumed they had
covered. In addition, she did not know whether to adopt a structural,
functional or communicative approach with them. When asked whether
she felt that the idea of a negotiated curriculum was idealistic, she replied:

> No, I agree with it. It's worked well with me before. I think of the
> curriculum as methodology as well as syllabus, and I've negotiated
> syllabus in the past rather than methodology, and successfully too.
> It's easier to see if methodology is being successful rather than
> syllabus.

Sally also suspected that her problems were compounded by the fact that she had been switched suddenly from working with newly-arrived immigrants to a group of learners who had already had at least one language programme and were considered to be ongoing. While there is some debate within the AMEP about the reality of the on-arrival/on-going distinction, for Sally it was certainly salient.

By the end of the week, Sally had decided that, rather than trying to negotiate with the learners, she would present them with a plan and ask them if it was acceptable to them.

A further problem related to student assessment. In the past, Sally had set objectives and used these to judge the learning outcomes, as well as evaluating her course. However, given the disparate nature of the group, and the fact that some of the students had already done many courses, she found it impossible to set objectives, and felt that the most she could do was to revise work which the students had already covered. Her frustration is evident in the following comment:

> At last I've got a class who could understand if I gave them a list of objectives, and I can't do it because of the disparate group – it's so frustrating! I don't know what they want, they haven't been able to tell me and I haven't been able to ask them in the right way. They may have ideas later, but in the meantime I have to do something.

For the next few weeks Sally decided to work on a weekly basis, giving out a fairly rigid plan at the beginning of the week, and seeing what the students thought at the end. At the beginning of each week, the students would also be given a paper that reviewed the previous week.

When asked at this early stage to nominate who she thought would be the most successful student at the end of the course, Sally replied:

> That's an interesting question. I know who'll be the most successful student – an ancient Chinese gentleman who was fluent in English as a youth and is now having it all reactivated. He's desperately keen to bring it all back, and he loves Australia and is interested in the culture. Motivation and interest in the target culture and being outgoing are the most important things.

At the End

By the end of the course, things had changed quite dramatically. Sally was a great deal more confident, and the students had been moulded into a much more tightly-knit group.

The composition of the class itself had changed slightly, with two of the students dropping out. These two had felt the class was too difficult for them, although Sally had tried to reassure them that this was not so. She reported that the two students in question had no confidence, and that she had been incapable of building up this confidence. Both apparently also had 'extreme' personality problems.

The most noticeable changes, apart from the more cohesive nature of the group, were in the attitude and motivation of the students. There was an interest and motivation in the work which had not been evident at the beginning of the course.

The change had been brought about by the teacher, in week four, deciding to conduct a fairly extensive survey of the students' attitudes towards the content, methodology, materials and class groupings. The students were asked to indicate what they found easy and what they found difficult, what they liked and what they disliked. The results revealed that half the class found things difficult and half found thing easy. However, none of the students found things either so easy or so difficult that they wanted to leave the class.

The survey was followed by an intensive counselling session, in which Sally followed up on the major points arising out of the survey. All students had given a low rating to pair work. In fact, it was the only thing they hated enough to want to stop. This was a real problem for Sally, as a great many classroom activities were based on group and pair work, so she decided to make pair work the focus of negotiation. She explained to them that she wanted to give them the maximum amount of practice and if they had difficulty then this was part of communicating and learning to communicate, and that they had to work it out.

In reviewing reaction of the students to the consultative process, she stated that:

> At first they were a bit stunned and amused at the teacher wanting them to give their opinions on content and methodology. I explained that I'd been worried because of the disparate levels, and that some things would be difficult for some learners and that I was very interested to know. They were really pleased to be consulted ... Explaining and giving the rationale is crucial.

As a result of the consultation process, all learners were quite prepared to continue with the pair work. Clarifying the rationale also made 'an incredible difference to how they went about the pair work. Before, they were really sluggish and reluctant – just going through the motions. Now they really get into it.'

In addition to the survey and consultation sessions, the group settled down of its own accord, which also greatly improved the classroom climate.

An additional factor concerned the difficulty level of the materials and activities set for the class. During the course of the first five weeks, Sally realised that the level was too high. Having been used to working with beginners, she assumed that because these were pre-intermediate/intermediate learners, they should be revising. Once the difficulty level of the work had been brought down, the classroom climate improved.

Even at the mid point in the course, and despite the fact that the group had settled down, Sally still had difficulty planning beyond a week ahead. She planned things on a weekly basis at a fairly general level and then did the detailed planning on a daily basis. As someone who generally liked to be well planned, she attributed this to her inexperience with the group, plus the disparate proficiency levels. At this point, she stated that the most important lesson she had learned in terms of curriculum was that it is not always possible to be completely well planned. She went on to state that:

> At first I found this very upsetting. I hate not knowing where I'm going, and in the past I've always had detailed plans with objectives and all the rest.

Despite the improvement in the group, Sally still found it impossible to write objectives. Given the disparate nature of the group, she found that different students got different things from a given task or activity.

The experience with the group confirmed her opinion that any sort of useful needs analysis could only be carried out once some sort of rapport had been established with the group, and that this might take five or six weeks. She felt that quite formal analysis with surveys and questionnaires were at least as useful as informal monitoring at this late stage in the course.

In terms of materials, at this stage she was finding the lack of suitable reading and writing materials for learners with low literacy skills a real problem.

When asked what was the most surprising or unexpected thing that she had learned during the course, she replied that she had never been so aware of the importance of affective factors to learning, that motivation and extra work on the part of some learners had led to incredible improvement. 'Two students work ten hours a day on their English and give me unsolicited homework. One student who was having literacy problems has improved out of sight.'

During the course, Sally spent about six hours in planning for her ten contact hours. A great deal of time was spent thinking. 'Once I've got my thoughts organised, I'm off. The thinking's the hard part.'

In general, she did comparatively little about developing the students' learning strategies, although she reported that they were all 'obsessed with their lack of ability to remember'. Thus, the focus for both teacher and students remained firmly on the development of language rather than learning skills.

Results and Conclusions

This study was designed to examine what happens when a national language programme abandons its centralised curriculum for a learner-centred model which requires the classroom practitioner to be the principal agent of curriculum development. The short answer to the research question posed at the beginning of the chapter is that such a move is likely to lead to a fragmentation of the curriculum, particularly when there are not concomitant changes to other aspects of the system such as professional development opportunities, administrative arrangements, counselling assessment and referral and general principles of curriculum management.

Conclusions Concerning Curriculum

One of the points which emerged most strongly from the study was the fact that continuity in language programmes is not just a curricular or pedagogical problem. It is an administrative, management and organisational problem as well as a counselling and curriculum-support problem. Many of the reasons advanced in interviews, and also comments made by teachers in Part C of the questionnaire on lack of continuity, are related to organisational constraints. In the case study, the teacher's difficulty in ensuring within-course continuity was due largely to the organisational decisions (and perhaps the lack of adequate or appropriate assessment and referral procedures) which led to the formation of an extremely disparate group. (In fact, it must be said that such disparate groups, while not the norm, are by no means unusual, particularly in smaller language centres.)

It also seems fairly obvious that if teachers are to be the ones responsible for developing the curriculum, they need the time, the skills and the support to do so. Support may include curriculum models and guidelines. It should also include counselling and bilingual support, and may include support from individuals acting in a curriculum advisory position. The provision of such support cannot be removed from, and must not be seen in isolation from, the curriculum.

If teachers are to be the principal agents of curriculum development, they need to develop a range of skills which go beyond classroom management and instruction. Curriculum development will therefore be largely a matter of appropriate staff development.

In many institutions, it is customary to identify teachers as 'experienced' or 'inexperienced' according to the number of years they have been teaching (a common cut-off figure seems to be four or five). However, it may well be that there is no such thing as an 'experienced' teacher, if by experienced is meant a teacher who can, at a moment's notice and with minimal support, plan, implement and evaluate a course in any area of the Program. This was demonstrated by the experience of Sally. It also emerged in interviews where only one or two per cent of teachers indicated that they would be able to teach in an unfamiliar area without support.

In general, there is a great deal of confusion over the term 'curriculum'. Many teachers see 'the curriculum' as a set of prescriptive statements about what 'should happen'. This makes any reference to curriculum matters by outsiders quite threatening. There is a need for the scope of curriculum to be expanded to include not only what 'should happen', but also what 'does happen'. Curriculum practice should thus be derived as much from successful practice as from statements of intent.

This, in fact, returns us to the point that the relationship between planning, teaching and learning is extremely complex. The notion that there is a simple equation between these three components of the curriculum (i.e. that 'what is planned' = 'what is taught' = 'what is learned') is naive, simplistic and misleading. It is crucial for those involved in course and programme evaluation to be aware of this complexity.

In terms of the provision of support, other teachers have the highest credibility in the eyes of practitioners. The practice of removing competent teachers from the classroom to be administrators or advisors results in an immediate drop in credibility. It may be more desirable to target practitioners who have expertise in a limited domain, e.g. 'literacy' or 'assessment', than as 'experts' across the total field of curriculum activity.

The amount that a teacher working alone can achieve is strictly limited. The best teacher-based curriculum development occurs as the result of team efforts, when groups of teachers with similar concerns or with similar students work together to develop a programme or course. Such collaboration may or may not include team teaching. While team teaching is recognised by teachers as being highly desirable, many reported that they were prevented from adopting a team approach by administrative and bureaucratic inflexibility.

In the past, within the AMEP, there has been a tendency for initiatives which have curricular implications to be introduced on a grand scale in an unsystematic way with very little monitoring and evaluation. The adoption of a learner-centred approach to curriculum is a case in point. Other examples include the development of self-access centres and the introduction of bilingual information officers. The same may well be said of plans to introduce counselling services, bilingual assistants and curriculum advisors. There is a great deal to be said for curriculum development to occur through small-scale case studies and action research projects which are adequately planned, closely monitored and properly evaluated, rather than through large-scale national initiatives. Teachers are certainly inclined to adopt an innovation which is the result of successful practice than an untested idea which is thrust upon them.

Many of the problems which are attributed to lack of curriculum continuity flow directly from the adoption of a learner-centred philosophy and the requirement, inherent in this philosophy, that the classroom practitioner be the principal agent of curriculum development. It may well be that a certain amount of discontinuity is inevitable; the price we pay for the chosen philosophy. There is certainly no single or simple solution.

In fact, lack of continuity manifests itself in many different ways which are partly a reflection of local conditions. As such, no national initiative can hope to ensure continuity. In a learner-centred system, where programmes will vary according to client needs, this has to happen at a local level. The best that educational administrators can hope to do is to provide a range of resources which may be utilised by individual centres for their own ends.

Conclusions Concerning Research

In this section, I should like to make a number of observations on the task of carrying out curriculum research and evaluation.

The first point to be made is that research and evaluation in the curriculum area is a high risk / high threat activity, stressful for both the researcher and those being researched. In order for the activity to be acceptable to those being researched, there is a need for openness on the part of the researcher. In particular, there is a need for objectives and methodology to be as explicit as possible. Those who provide data through interviews, questionnaires and so on should retain control of the data, even if, at times, this means that some of the data are unable to be used.

It is generally accepted that research and evaluation projects are undertaken to provide useful information for practitioners. If it is intended that the results of research be reflected in future curriculum activity, the research methods which are adopted have to have validity in the eyes of practitioners. In the case of the present study, it was the case that qualitative methods had much more validity than quantitative methods.

In fact, a variety of data-gathering procedures need to be employed if anything like a complete picture is to emerge. The data obtained from one method sometimes conflicts with that of another, and a balanced and accurate view will result only if all the results are seen in concert (see also Lett and Shaw 1986).

It is also necessary to obtain information for a variety of sources. In the present instance, a very different picture of curriculum issues, problems and solutions emerged from different stake-holders within the Program. Thus, senior administration and management tended to locate problems of continuity within courses, whereas teachers tended to identify discontinuities between courses. In another instance, one group of teachers gave a low rating on the questionnaire to the suggestion that a certificate of ESL be developed as a way of systematising the curriculum. However, the same group in an interview were much more positive about the certificate suggestion. When challenged on this, they rationalised it in terms of their negative reaction to the questionnaire.

Summary

We have seen through this study of teachers as curriculum developers a reinforcement of many of the points made in the preceding chapters. We have seen that, in a learner-centred system the teacher must, of necessity, be the principal agent of curriculum development. We have also seen that, without appropriate time, skills and support, teachers will have a great deal of difficulty fulfilling their potential as curriculum developers. Finally we have seen the complexity of the curriculum development process in action.

10.3   Future Directions

For most of its history, language teaching has been at the mercy of pronouncements from self-styled experts. It has suffered from the misapplication and misinterpretation of theory and research from other disciplines. In recent years, these other disciplines have included theoretical linguistics and its various applied offspring, behavioural, cognitive and humanistic psychology, first- and second-language acquisition, sociology, information theory, systems theory and educational technology. It has also been at the mercy of numerous applied linguists who have foisted their frequently untested or inadequately tested theories on the profession. This has led to a number of undesirable outcomes. Instead of a cautious programme of research and development, the profession has been characterised by a series of fads and fashions. Armchair speculation has spawned competing untested (and sometimes untestable) assertions about the nature of second-language development inside and outside the classroom.

The general lack of systematic study of classroom learning and the sorts of classroom-centred research advocated in the previous chapter have led, amongst other things, to the proliferation of competing methodologies. These include 'mainstream' methodologies such as audiolingualism and communicative language teaching as well as 'fringe' varieties such as Total Physical Response, the Silent Way, the Natural Approach, Suggestopedia, Community Language Learning and SCAV. These 'work' to a greater or lesser extent, depending on the attitudes of the students, the competence of the teacher and the context in which the teaching–learning occurs. In fact, we have yet to devise a methodology which is incapable of teaching anybody anything, so claims by devotees that Method X 'works' are of little real value.

The point is that these methods, more often than not, are based on the misapplication of theories from other fields, have not been systematically validated over an extended period, and have been developed partly in reaction to what has gone before. Thus, we have the familiar 'pendulum' effect.

While most teachers are highly professional, as the studies documented in these pages attest, the 'fads and fashions' approach has led many teachers to adopt an extremely suspicious attitude towards theoretical pronouncements of any kind. There is also the contrasting type of teacher who enthusiastically embraces one approach and defends it valiantly against all criticism and challenge.

The most urgent need is for the profession to adopt a more rigorous approach to the planning, implementation and evaluation of the curriculum. An important aspect of this will be the generation and testing of hypotheses about language learning and teaching.

The sceptic might claim that this was tried and found wanting in the 1960s, when large-scale, but largely inconclusive, 'method' comparisons were attempted. However, the failure of these experiments does not necessarily mean that experimentation, particularly that of the illuminative kind, has nothing of value to contribute to curriculum development. In fact, it may well have been that a qualitative dimension to the research conducted in the 1960s would have revealed uncontrolled variables contaminating the research (see for example Long 1983).

Perhaps the most pressing need is to develop a more rigorously-formulated and empirically-based approach to language proficiency. This is a daunting task because it will involve quantifying a variety of linguistic and non-linguistic variables each of which interact in complex ways. (It may, in fact, transpire that these interactions are idiosyncratic and therefore ultimately non-quantifiable.)

The complexity of quantifying language proficiency is captured in the following extract from a paper on proficiency profiles.

> There has been talk of late about the development of 'proficiency profiles', as an alternative to the relatively imprecise proficiency rating scales (Campbell 1985). However, unless such profiles are empirically derived, they are unlikely to be any more satisfactory than the rating scales they are intended to replace. From the discussion in the preceding section, we know that proficiency

> consists of a plurality of factors, which interact in complex ways.
> Profiles would need to identify and articulate these diverse factors
> and give some indication of how they interrelated in real
> communication.
>
> (Nunan 1987b: 166)

At the very least, it is likely that proficiency profiles would need to
be constructed along two dimensions. One dimension would be what
might be called 'subject factors' (i.e. factors relating to the learner) and
would include such things as syntactic and morphological mastery, pronunciation, fluency, sociocultural knowledge, lexical knowledge, subject-
matter knowledge, and so on. The other dimension could be termed
'task factors' and these would be located within the task itself. They
would include degree of contextual support, cognitive demand, amount
of assistance provided, psycholinguistic processing difficulty and degree
of stress.

If those advocating the development of profiles intend that they be
stable indices of the learner's current state of development, then there
is bound to be disappointment. Given the complex interaction between
'subject' and 'task' factors, the profiles themselves are likely to be highly
unstable. Thus, the 'subject profile' for a given learner might look quite
different from one task to another, according to the degree to which
'task' factors influence the ability of the learner to carry out the task.

In order to clarify this point, let us consider an example. Let us assume
that reasonably precise instruments for measuring the mobilisation of
the subject factors of syntactic mastery, pronunciation, fluency, discourse, sociocultural knowledge and subject-matter knowledge have been
developed and empirically validated. The instruments are then used to
measure the performance of Subject A on Task X, which results in the
profile shown in Figure 10.2:

FIGURE 10.2

KEY
1 syntax
2 pronunciation
3 fluency
4 discourse
5 socio-cultural knowledge
6 subject-matter knowledge

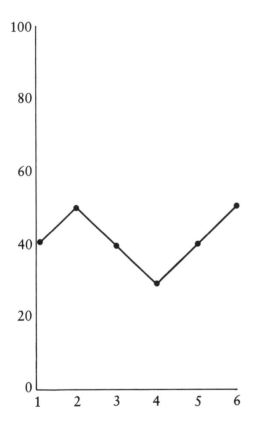

On Task Y, however, in which the task factors such as processing difficulty and contextual support are different, Subject A may have the profile
shown in Figure 10.3.

FIGURE 10.3

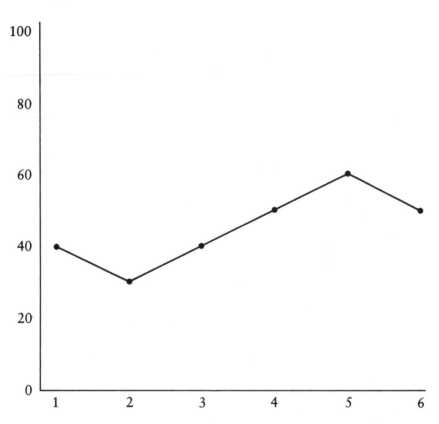

The hypothesis suggested here, then, is that proficiency profiles must take into consideration two sets of factors which will interact in complex ways to make the profile for any given learner unstable. This hypothesis needs to be empirically tested to estimate the degree of instability. The variability of different learner profiles also needs to be computed. If there is reasonable correlation in the direction and magnitude of variability across tasks, generalisations can start to be made.

(Nunan 1987b: 167–8)

10.4   Conclusion

In this concluding section I shall review some of the major points which have emerged during the course of this study, and shall attempt to draw together the major themes.

The work has essentially been about the development of language curricula within the general learner-centred philosophy which emerged as an offspring of communicative language learning. A central tenet of the work is that a learner-centred philosophy entails differentiated curricula for different learner types, and that within educational systems subscribing to such a philosophy it is the classroom practitioner who will bear the major burden for curriculum development. During the course of the study, we have seen how teachers have responded to the challenge of being involved in all phases of curriculum development.

Chapter 1 provided an overview of the book as a whole. In Chapter 2, some general curriculum models were described, and a model was argued for which is both integrative and systematic. It was suggested that, minimally, such a model would include principles and procedures for planning, implementing and evaluating the following curriculum elements: initial and ongoing needs analysis; content selection and gradation (including goal and objective setting); methodology (which will include the selection and gradation of learning activities and materials); and, finally, monitoring, assessment and evaluation. It was further suggested that decisions relating to each of these elements may be made during the course of programme delivery (i.e. a 'ballistic' approach to curriculum development was specifically rejected.

Another major issue to emerge was the complexity of the relationship between planning, teaching and learning. In the past, particularly with the dominance of Tyler's (1949) 'rational curriculum model', it was assumed that there was a simple equation between planning intention, teaching reality and learning outcome. Such an assumption greatly over-simplifies and distorts what really happens in the teaching–learning process, and leads to unrealistic expectations. It also engenders a sense of failure and frustration in teaching when what is planned is not always translated into learning outcomes. While it is desirable to attempt to bring planned objectives and learning outcomes into alignment, a mismatch between intention and reality should not necessarily be attributed to shortcomings on the part of the teacher. In fact, only some of many alternative reasons for learning failure have been documented in the preceding pages. In addition, as Allwright (1986) has pointed out, the fact that what has been taught is not always learned does not mean that the effort on the part of teachers and learners has been wasted. In fact, unanticipated outcomes may sometimes be as valuable as those which were anticipated.

In addition to the development of language skills, it has been argued that a learner-centred approach will be concerned with the development of and sensitisation of learners to their role as learners. In consequence, while one set of goals and objectives will relate to the development of language skills, a parallel set will relate to the development of learning skills. A focus on the development of learner autonomy and independent learning skills will be particularly important in systems which can offer the learner only short-term courses.

Within this work, I have been concerned to develop a comprehensive view of curriculum. The curriculum is thus seen as much more than a set of initial planning procedures and content specifications (the 'what should be'). It is an integrated system which gives prominence to what actually happens during the course of programme delivery. The curriculum is thus seen as an amalgamation of intention and reality.

In order to provide a sounder basis for curriculum development, I have advocated a greater use of empirical research, particularly classroom-centred research. In the current work, numerous small-scale studies were conducted specifically to illustrate the points under investigation, and to give a sharper focus to the work as a whole. These culminate in the large-scale investigation of the 'teacher as curriculum developer', the results of which are set out in this final chapter. The study demonstrates that, in a language programme based on a learner-centred philosophy, teachers have been prepared to redefine their roles and to take on many of the tasks previously seen as the province of curriculum specialists. However, the study also demonstrated the complexities and difficulties inherent in this redefined role, and underlined the crucial importance of having adequate support resources, particularly appropriate administrative and managerial support, if a localised curriculum model is to operate effectively. Thus, while teachers are prepared to accept responsibility for curriculum development, and to see themselves as prime agents in the curriculum process, they can face great difficulty if the added burden of their redefined role is not recognised.

Above all, I have tried to take an educational perspective on the development of language curricula. While theoretical linguistics will continue to be an important base discipline, it is important that it not be seen as the only discipline which has anything of value to contribute to decision making on what, how and when to teach. While the learning of a second language has unique aspects, it is not so unique as to have nothing to gain from general educational theory, practice and research.

Finally, in the preceding section, a call is made for more empirical research into language learning and teaching. While there is by no means universal agreement amongst them, some second-language acquisition researchers have provided us with useful methodological models in their theoretically- and empirically-motivated investigations. Hopefully, similar work in the future will provide us with a firmer foundation than the speculative approach which has thus far dominated much of the literature on the language curriculum.

References

Alcorso, C. and M. Kalantzis (1985) *The Learning Process and Being a Learner in the AMEP*, report to the Committee of Review of the Adult Migrant Education Program, Department of Immigration and Ethnic Affairs, Canberra.

Allwright, R. (1986) 'Making sense of instruction: What's the problem?', *PALM*, 1, 2, University of Michigan.

Asher, J. (1977) *Learning Another Language Through Actions: The Complete Teacher's Guide*. Los Gatos, Ca.: Sky Oaks Productions.

Bachman, L. and M. Mack (1986) 'A causal analysis of learner characteristics and second language proficiency', paper presented at the Twentieth Annual TESOL Convention, Anaheim, California.

Bartlett, L. and J. Butler (1985) *The Planned Curriculum and Being a Curriculum Planner in the Adult Migrant Education Program*, report to the Committee of Review of the Adult Migrant Education Program, Department of Immigration and Ethnic Affairs, Canberra.

Beretta, A. (1986a) 'Toward a methodology of ESL program evaluation', *TESOL Quarterly*, 20, 1.

Beretta, A. (1986b) 'Program-fair language teaching evaluation', *TESOL Quarterly*, 20, 3.

Breen, M. and C. Candlin (1980) 'The essentials of a communicative curriculum in language teaching', *Applied Linguistics*, 1, 2.

Brindley, G. (1984) *Needs Analysis and Objective Setting in the Adult Migrant Education Program*. Sydney: NSW Adult Migrant Education Service.

Brindley, G. (1986) *The Assessment of Second Language Proficiency: Issues and Approaches*. Adelaide: National Curriculum Resource Centre.

Brink, A., H. Frazer, H. Mullins and H. Reade (1985) *Let's Try to Do it Better*, report to the Committee of Review of the Adult Migrant Education Program, Department of Immigration and Ethnic Affairs, Canberra.

Brumfit, C. (1984) *Communicative Methodology in Language Teaching: The Roles of Fluency and Accuracy*. Cambridge: Cambridge University Press.

Brundage, D.H. and D. MacKeracher (1980) *Adult Learning Principles and their Application to Program Planning*. Ontario: Ontario Institute for Studies in Education.

Burnett, L. and J. Hitchen (1985) *Crossover Course*. Sydney: NSW Adult Migrant Education Service.

Burton, J. and D. Nunan (1986) 'The effect of learners' theories on language learning', Applied Linguistics Association of Australia Annual Conference, Adelaide University, August 1986.

CAL (1983) *From the Classroom to the Workplace: Teaching ESL to Adults.* Washington: Center for Applied Linguistics.

Candlin, C. and C. Edelhoff (1982) *Challenges: Teacher's Guide.* London: Longman.

Carroll, B. (1981) *Testing Communicative Performance.* Oxford: Pergamon.

Carver, D. and L. Dickinson (1982) 'Learning to be self-directed', in M. Geddes and G. Sturtridge (eds), *Individualisation.* Modern English Publications.

Chaudron, C. (1988) *Second Language Classrooms: Research on Teaching and Learning.* Cambridge: Cambridge University Press.

Chomsky, N. (1965) *Aspects of the Theory of Syntax.* Cambridge Mass.: M.I.T. Press.

Clark, J. (1985a) 'Curriculum renewal', Keynote Address to the Australian Association of Applied Linguistics, Griffith University, Brisbane, August 1985.

Clark, J. (1985b) *The Australian Language Levels Project: Working Papers.* Adelaide: Multicultural Education Centre.

Corbel, C. (1985) 'The "action sequence" approach to course design'. *Prospect,* 1, 1.

Day, R. (ed.) (1985) *Talking to Learn.* Rowley: Newbury House.

Diller, K. (1978) *The Language Teaching Controversy.* Rowley: Newbury House.

Dinsmore, D. (1985) 'Waiting for Godot in the classroom', *ELT Journal,* 39, 4.

Dubin, F. and E. Olshtain (1986) *Course Design.* Cambridge: Cambridge University Press.

Economou, D. (1985) *Coffee Break: Understanding Australian Casual Conversation.* Adelaide: National Curriculum Resource Centre.

Ellis, R. (1985) *Understanding Second Language Acquisition.* Oxford: Oxford University Press.

Eltis, K. and B. Low (1985) *A Review of the Teaching Process in the Adult Migrant Education Program,* report to the Committee of Review of the Adult Migrant Education Program, Department of Immigration and Ethnic Affairs, Canberra.

Gregg, K. (1984) 'Krashen's Monitor and Occam's Razor', *Applied Linguistics,* 5, 2.

Gronlund, N. (1981) *Measurement and Evaluation in Education.* New York: Macmillan.

Halliday, M.A.K. (1973) *Explorations in the Functions of Language.* London: Edward Arnold.

Halliday, M.A.K. (1975) *Learning How to Mean.* London: Edward Arnold.

Halliday, M.A.K. (1978) *Language as Social Semiotic: Social Interpretation of Language and Meaning.* London: Edward Arnold.

Higgs, T.V. (ed.) (1984) *Teaching for Proficiency, the Organising Principle.* Lincolnwood: National Textbook Company.

Howatt, A. (1984) *A History of English Language Teaching.* Oxford: Oxford University Press.

Hunkins, F.P. (1980) *Curriculum Development: Program Improvement.* Columbus, Ohio: Charles E. Merrill Publishing Co.

Hyltenstam, K. and M. Pienemann (1985) *Modelling and Assessing Second Language Acquisition*. Clevedon: Multilingual Matters.

Ingram, D. (1981) *Methodology*. Canberra: Department of Immigration and Ethnic Affairs.

Ingram, D. (1984) *Australian Second Language Proficiency Ratings*. Canberra: Department of Immigration and Ethnic Affairs.

Johnston, M. (1985) *Syntactic and Morphological Progressions in Learner English*. Canberra: Department of Immigration and Ethnic Affairs.

Jones, M. and R. Moar (1985) *Listen to Australia*. Sydney: NSW Adult Migrant Education Service.

Kemmis, S. and R. McTaggart (1982) *The Action Research Planner*. Victoria: Deakin University Press.

Kerr, J. (ed.) (1968) *Changing the Curriculum*. London: University of London Press.

Knowles, M. (1983) *The Adult Learner: A Neglected Species*. Houston: Gulf Publishing Company.

Krashen, S. (1981) *Second Language Acquisition and Second Language Learning*. Oxford: Pergamon.

Krashen, S. (1982) *Principles and Practice in Second Language Acquisition*. Oxford: Pergamon.

Krashen, S. and T. Terrell (1983) *The Natural Approach*. Oxford: Pergamon.

Lawton, D. (1973) *Social Change, Educational Theory and Curriculum Planning*. London: Hodder and Stoughton.

Lett, J. and P. Shaw (1986) 'Combining qualitative and quantitative program evaluation: A research report', paper presented at the Twentieth Annual TESOL Convention, Anaheim, California.

Littlewood, W. (1981) *Communicative Language Teaching: an Introduction*. Cambridge: Cambridge University Press.

Long, M.H. (1981) 'Input, interaction and second language acquisition', in H. Winitz (ed.), *Native Language and Foreign Language Acquisition*. New York: New York Academy of Sciences.

Long, M.H. (1983) 'Process and product in ESL program evaluation', *TESOL Quarterly*, 18, 3.

Long, M.H. (1985) 'A role for instruction in second language acquisition', in K. Hyltenstam and M. Pienemann (eds), *Modelling and Assessing Second Language Acquisition*. Clevedon: Multilingual Matters.

Long, M.H. and G. Crookes (1986) 'Intervention points in second language classroom processes', *Working Papers*, 5, 2. Department of English as a Second Language, University of Hawaii.

Long, M.H. and P. Porter (1985) 'Group work, interlanguage talk and second language acquisition', *TESOL Quarterly*, 19, 2.

Long, M.H. and C. Sato (1983) 'Classroom foreigner talk discourse: forms and functions of teachers' questions', in Seliger and Long (eds), 1983.

Macdonald, B. and R. Walker (1975) 'Case study and the social philosophy of educational research', *Cambridge Journal of Education*, 5, 1.

Macdonald-Ross, M. (1975) 'Behavioural objectives: a critical review', in M. Golby (ed.) *Curriculum Design*. London: Croom Helm.

Mager, R. (1975) *Preparing Instructional Objectives*. Paolo Alto: Fearon Publishers.

Montgomery, C. and M. Eisenstein (1985) 'Real reality revisited: an experimental communicative course in ESL', *TESOL Quarterly*, 19, 2.

Morrow, K. (1985) 'The evaluation of tests of communicative performance'. *Prospect*, 1, 2.

Munby, J. (1978) *Communicative Syllabus Design*. Cambridge: Cambridge University Press.

Nicholas, H. (1985) 'Interactive strategies, "input" and "output"', *ATESOL 4th Summer School Proceedings: Volume 1*. Sydney: ATESOL.

Nunan, D. (1985a) *Language Teaching Course Design: Trends and Issues*. Adelaide: National Curriculum Resource Centre.

Nunan, D. (1985b) 'Using objective grids in planning language courses', *Prospect*, 1, 2.

Nunan, D. (1986a) 'Communicative language teaching: the learner's view', paper presented at the RELC Regional Seminar Singapore, 21–26 April 1986.

Nunan, D. (1986b) 'The learner-centred curriculum: principles and procedures', *Working Papers*, 5, 2. Department of English as a Second Language, University of Hawaii.

Nunan, D. (1986c) 'Can the language classroom ever be truly communicative?', Distinguished Scholar Series, University of the Pacific, California, March 1986.

Nunan, D. (1987a) *Guidelines for the Development of Curriculum Resources*. Adelaide: National Curriculum Resource Centre.

Nunan, D. (1987b) 'The ghost in the machine: an examination of the concept of language proficiency', *Prospect*, 2, 3.

Nunan, D. (1988) *Syllabus Design*. Oxford: Oxford University Press.

Nunan, D. and G. Brindley (1986) 'A practical framework for learner-centred curriculum development', paper presented at the Twentieth Annual TESOL Convention, Anaheim, California.

O'Grady, C. and G. Kang (1985) *Use of the Learner's First Language in Adult Migrant Education*. Sydney: Adult Migrant Education Service.

Oller, J. (1979) *Language Tests at School*. London: Longman.

Omaggio, A., P. Eddy, L. McKim and A. Pfannkuche (1979) 'Looking at the results', in J. Phillips (ed.), *Building on Experience: Building for Success*. Skokie: National Textbook Company.

Oskarsson, M. (1980) *Approaches to Self-Assessment in Foreign Language Learning*. Oxford: Pergamon.

Parlett, M. and D. Hamilton (1983) 'Evaluation as illumination', in L. Bartlett and S. Kemmis (eds), *Naturalistic Observation*. Victoria: Deakin University Press.

Pienemann, M. (1985) 'Learnability and syllabus construction', in K. Hyltenstam and M. Pienemann (eds), *Modelling and Assessing Second Language Acquisition*. Clevedon: Multilingual Matters.

Porter, P. (1985) 'How learners talk to each other: input and interaction in task-centred discussions', in R. Day (ed.), *Talking to Learn: Conversations in Second Language Acquisition*. Rowley: Newbury House.

Prabhu, N. (1983) 'Procedural syllabuses', paper presented at the RELC Regional Seminar, Singapore, April 1983.

Quinn, T. (1984) 'Functional approaches in language pedagogy', *Annual Review of Applied Linguistics*. Cambridge: Cambridge University Press.

Rea, P. (1985) 'Language testing and the communicative language teaching curriculum', in Y.P. Lee, C.Y.Y. Fok, R. Lord and G. Low (eds), *New Directions in Language Testing*. Oxford: Pergamon.

Richards, J. (1984) 'Language curriculum development', *RELC Journal*, 15, 1.

Richards, J. (1985a) 'Planning for proficiency', *Prospect*, 1, 2.

Richards, J. (1985b) 'Conversational competence through role play activities', *RELC Journal*, 16, 1.

Richards, J., J. Platt and H. Weber (1985) *A Dictionary of Applied Linguistics*. London: Longman.

Richards, J. and T. Rodgers (1986) *Approaches and Methods in Language Teaching*. Cambridge: Cambridge University Press.

Richterich, R. (1972) *A Model for the Definition of Language Needs*. Strasbourg: Council of Europe.

Richterich, R. (1975) 'The analysis of language needs: illusion – pretext – reality', in *Modern Language Learning by Adults, Education and Culture* No. 28, Strasbourg: Council of Europe.

Richterich, R. and J-L. Chancerel (1978) *Identifying the Needs of Adults Learning a Foreign Language*. Strasbourg: Council of Europe.

Rivers, W.M. (1983) *Communicating Naturally in a Second Language*. Cambridge: Cambridge University Press.

Rowntree, D. (1981) *Developing Courses for Students*. London: McGraw Hill (UK).

RSA (1983) *The Communicative Use of English as a Foreign Language*. London: Royal Society of Arts.

Savignon, S. and M. Berns (eds) (1984) *Initiatives in Communicative Language Teaching*. Reading, Mass.: Addison-Wesley.

Seliger, H. (1983) 'Learner interaction in the classroom and its effect on language acquisition', in Seliger and Long (eds), (1983).

Seliger, H. and M.H. Long (eds) (1983) *Classroom Oriented Research in Second Language Acquisition*. Rowley: Newbury House.

Shavelson, R.J. and P. Stern (1981) 'Research on teachers' pedagogical thoughts, judgments and behaviour', *Review of Educational Research*, 51, 4.

Shaw, J. and G. Dowsett (1986) *The Evaluation Process in the Adult Migrant Education Program: The Report of the National Course Reporting Study*. Adelaide: National Curriculum Resource Centre.

Slade, D. (1986) *Teaching Casual Conversation*. Adelaide: National Curriculum Resource Centre.

Stenhouse, L. (1975) *An Introduction to Curriculum Research and Development*. London: Heinemann.

Stern, H.H. (1983) *Fundamental Concepts of Language Teaching*. Oxford: Oxford University Press.

Swain, M. (1985) 'Communicative competence: some roles of comprehensible input and comprehensible output in its development', in S. Gass and C. Madden (eds), *Input in Second Language Acquisition*. Rowley: Newbury House.

Swaffar, J., K. Arens and M. Morgan (1982) 'Teacher classroom practices: redefining method as task hierarchy', *Modern Language Journal*, 66, 1.

Taba, H. (1962) *Curriculum Development: Theory and Practice.* New York: Harcourt Brace.

Tyler, R. (1949) *Basic Principles of Curriculum and Instruction.* New York: Harcourt Brace.

Valette, R. and R. Disick (1972) *Modern Language Performance Objectives and Individualisation.* New York: Harcourt Brace.

van Ek, J. and L.G. Alexander (1980) *Threshold Level English.* Oxford: Pergamon.

van Lier, L. (1988) *The Classroom and the Language Learner.* London: Longman.

Varonis, E. and S. Gass (1983) 'Target language input from non-native speakers', paper presented at the Seventeenth Annual TESOL Convention, Toronto.

Vollmer, H. and F. Sang (1983) 'Competing hypotheses about second language ability: a plea for caution', in J. Oller (ed.), *Issues in Language Testing Research.* Rowley: Newbury House.

Watts, B. (1985) *Being a Teacher in the AMEP*, report to the Committee of Review of the Adult Migrant Education Program, Department of Immigration and Ethnic Affairs, Canberra.

Wheeler, D. (1967) *Curriculum Processes.* London: University of London Press.

Widdowson, H.G. (1978) *Teaching Language as Communication.* Oxford: Oxford University Press.

Widdowson, H.G. (1979) *Explorations in Applied Linguistics.* Oxford: Oxford University Press.

Widdowson, H.G. (1983) *Learning Purpose and Language Use.* Oxford: Oxford University Press.

Widdowson, H.G. (1987) 'Aspects of syllabus design', in M. Tickoo (ed.), *Language Syllabuses: State of the Art.* Singapore: Regional Language Centre.

Wilkins, D. (1972) *Linguistics in Language Teaching.* London: Edward Arnold.

Wilkins, D. (1976) *Notional Syllabuses.* London: Oxford University Press.

Willing, K. (1985) *Learning Styles in Adult Migrant Education.* Sydney: NSW Adult Migrant Education Service.

Winitz, H. (ed.) (1981) *The Comprehension Approach to Foreign Language Instruction.* Rowley: Newbury House.

Yalden, J. (1983) *The Communicative Syllabus: Evolution, Design and Implementation.* Oxford: Pergamon.

Young, M. (1971) *Knowledge and Control.* London: Collier Macmillan.

Appendix

The following questionnaires have been adapted from Brindley (1984)

We would like you to tell us which of the following uses of English are important *for you.*
Please put an X in the box beside each to tell us if you think it is 'Very Useful', 'Useful', 'Not Useful'.

		Very Useful	Useful	Not Useful
	Do you want to improve your English so that you can:			
1	Tell people about yourself.	☐	☐	☐
2	Tell people about your family.	☐	☐	☐
3	Tell people about your job.	☐	☐	☐
4	Tell people about your education.	☐	☐	☐
5	Tell people about your interests.	☐	☐	☐
6	Use buses/trains/ferries.	☐	☐	☐
7	Find new places in the city.	☐	☐	☐
8	Speak to tradespeople.	☐	☐	☐
9	Speak to your landlord or real estate agent.	☐	☐	☐
10	Buy furniture or appliances for your home.	☐	☐	☐
11	Deal with door-to-door salesmen.	☐	☐	☐
12	Communicate with your children/grandchildren	☐	☐	☐
13	Receive telephone calls.	☐	☐	☐
14	Make telephone calls.	☐	☐	☐
15	Do further study.	☐	☐	☐
16	Get information about courses, schools etc.	☐	☐	☐
17	Enrol in courses.	☐	☐	☐
18	Get information about the NSW Education System.	☐	☐	☐
19	Help children with school work.	☐	☐	☐
20	Apply for a job.	☐	☐	☐
21	Get information about a job.	☐	☐	☐
22	Go to the CES.	☐	☐	☐

23 Attend interviews. ☐ ☐ ☐
24 Join sporting or social clubs. ☐ ☐ ☐
25 Join hobby or interest groups. ☐ ☐ ☐
26 Watch TV. ☐ ☐ ☐
27 Listen to the radio. ☐ ☐ ☐
28 Read newspapers/books/magazines. ☐ ☐ ☐
29 Give/accept/refuse invitations. ☐ ☐ ☐
30 Make travel arrangements. ☐ ☐ ☐
31 Talk to your boss. ☐ ☐ ☐
32 Talk to doctors/hospital staff. ☐ ☐ ☐
33 Talk to neighbours. ☐ ☐ ☐
34 Talk to your children's teachers. ☐ ☐ ☐
35 Talk to officials, e.g.
    Immigration/CES. ☐ ☐ ☐
36 Talk to English-speaking friends. ☐ ☐ ☐
37 Get information about goods you
    want to buy and services. ☐ ☐ ☐
38 Complain about or return goods. ☐ ☐ ☐
39 Arrange credit/hire-purchase/lay-by. ☐ ☐ ☐

*From this list choose five you want to learn *first*.

1 ....

2 ....

3 ....

4 ....

5 ....

How do you like learning?
Put a circle around your answer.

a) In class do you like learning

    1 individually?   YES/NO
    2 in pairs?   YES/NO
    3 in small groups?   YES/NO
    4 in one large group?   YES/NO

b) Do you want to do homework?   YES/NO

If so, how much time have you got for homework
outside class hours?

.... hours a day

or .... hours a week

How would you like to spend this time?

1 Preparing for the next class? YES/NO

2 Reviewing the day's work? YES/NO

3 Doing some kind of activity based on your personal
experience, work experience or interests? YES/NO

c) Do you want to

1 spend all your learning time in the classroom? YES/NO

or...

2 spend some time in the classroom and some time practising
your English with people outside? YES/NO

3 spend some time in the classroom and some time getting
to know your city and the Australian way of life, e.g. by
visiting Parliament, government offices, migrant resource
centres, places of interest, work entertainment and so on? YES/NO

d) Do you like learning

1 by memory? YES/NO

2 by problem solving? YES/NO

3 by getting information for yourself? YES/NO

4 by listening? YES/NO

5 by reading? YES/NO

6 by copying from the board? YES/NO

7 by listening and taking notes? YES/NO

8 by reading and making notes? YES/NO

9 by repeating what you hear? YES/NO

Put a cross next to the three things that
you find most useful.

e) When you speak do you want to be corrected

1 immediately, in front of everyone? YES/NO

or...

2 later, at the end of the activity, in front of everyone? YES/NO

3 later, in private? YES/NO

f) Do you mind if other students sometimes correct your
written work? YES/NO

Do you mind if the teacher sometimes asks you to
correct your own work? YES/NO

⋙→

g) Do you like learning from

    1 television/video/films?   YES/NO
    2 radio?   YES/NO
    3 tapes/cassettes? (e.g. language lab, language masters,
      cassette players)   YES/NO
    4 written material   YES/NO
    5 the blackboard?   YES/NO
    6 pictures/posters?   YES/NO

h) Do you find these activities useful?

    1 Role play   YES/NO
    2 Language games   YES/NO
    3 Songs   YES/NO
    4 Talking with and listening to other students   YES/NO
    5 Memorising conversations/dialogues   YES/NO
    6 Getting information from guest speakers   YES/NO
    7 Getting information from planned visits   YES/NO

i) How do you like to find out how much
    your English is improving?

        By ....

    1 written tasks set by the teacher?   YES/NO
    2 oral language samples taken and assessed by the teacher?   YES/NO
    3 checking your own progress by making tapes, listening
      to them critically and comparing them?   YES/NO
    4 devising your own written tasks for completion by
      yourself and other students?   YES/NO
    5 seeing if you can use the language you have learnt in
      real-life situations?   YES/NO

j) Do you get a sense of satisfaction from:

    1 having your work graded?   YES/NO
    2 being told that you have made progress?   YES/NO
    3 feeling more confident in situations that you found
      difficult before?   YES/NO

Index

Index